Lothian

Edited by Mark Richardson

 Young**Writers**

First published in Great Britain in 2008 by:
Young Writers
Remus House
Coltsfoot Drive
Peterborough
PE2 9JX
Telephone: 01733 890066
Website: www.youngwriters.co.uk

SB ISBN 978-1 84431 658 8

Foreword

Young Writers was established in 1991 and has been passionately devoted to the promotion of reading and writing in children and young adults ever since. The quest continues today. Young Writers remains as committed to the nurturing of poetic and literary talent as ever.

This year's Young Writers competition has proven as vibrant and dynamic as ever and we are delighted to present a showcase of the best poetry from across the UK and in some cases overseas. Each poem has been selected from a wealth of *Little Laureates 2008* entries before ultimately being published in this, our seventeenth primary school poetry series.

Once again, we have been supremely impressed by the overall quality of the entries we have received. The imagination, energy and creativity which has gone into each young writer's entry made choosing the poems a challenging and often difficult but ultimately hugely rewarding task - the general high standard of the work submitted ensured this opportunity to bring their poetry to a larger appreciative audience.

We sincerely hope you are pleased with this final collection and that you will enjoy *Little Laureates 2008 Lothian* for many years to come.

Contents

Ewan Lennie (10)	38
Gerard Smillie (10)	38
Kyle Black (9)	39
Kerry McDonald (9)	39
Alexander Ferguson (8)	39
Chloe Hunter (9)	40

Echline Primary School
Katie O'Rourke (7)	40
Hamish Robinson (7)	41
David MacNeill (7)	41
Lucy Guthrie (7)	42
Catherine Kelly (7)	42
Amy Rankin (7)	43
Samantha Millar (7)	43
Hannah Baillie (7)	44
Chloë Sutherland (7)	44
Michelle Peden (7)	44
James Ferguson (7)	45

Flora Stevenson Primary School
Peter Robertson (9)	45
Eilidh Cameron (11)	46
Varshini Vijayakumar (11)	47
Umar Majid (11)	47
Harriet Johnston (10)	48
Jennifer Kerr (11)	48
Fiona Begg (10)	49
Sean Carson (9)	49

Juniper Green Primary School
Katherine Allan & Ione Drummond (11)	50
Sarah Dunn & Lauren McCabe	50
Fintan Purcell & Alistair Gordon (11)	51
Evan Richards & Connor Ratcliffe (11)	51
Murray Drummond & Victor Pilard (11)	52
Fahad Iqbal & Andrew McNicoll (11)	53
Phillipa Lumsden & Matthew Miller (11)	54

St Cuthbert's RC Primary School, Edinburgh

St Mary's Music School, Edinburgh

St Mary's Primary School, Bonnyrigg

St Ninian's RC Primary School, Livingston

Thomas McKeon (10)	70
Emily Daly (10)	71
Del Imrie (10)	71
John Heaney (8)	72
Kerri Mackay (9)	72
Karina Carroll (8)	72
Elliott Young (9)	73
Morgan Finlay (9)	73
Chantelle MacLean (8)	73
Becky Findlay (8)	74
Keanu Sneddon (8)	74
Alicia Turner (8)	74
Jordan More (12)	75
Ariana Hardie (8)	75
Sophie Wells (8)	75
Lewis Mulholland (9)	76
Cameron Russell (9)	76
Keri Gibson (8)	77
Ciaran McWalter (8)	77
Geena Reilly	78
Rhys Nixon (8)	78
Hugh Hardie (9)	79
Lauren Gilhooley (8)	79
Aidan Craig (8)	79
Eilidh Clark (8)	80
Ciaran McNeil (10)	80
Natasha Imrie (9)	80
Frank Declan McAlister (10)	81
Sheonaid Carlin (11)	81
Lee Francis McIlhone (10)	81
Natasha Reid (9)	82
James Alexander Bethell (11)	82
Robert McDonald (11)	82
Courtney Cook (10)	83
Annabelle Urquhart (10)	83
Ciaran Kelly (9)	83
Joe Helanor (10)	84
Lisa Harkins (11)	84
Paul Ewins (11)	84
Martin Hughes (9)	85
Jane Ewins (9)	85
Daniel Rolfe (9)	85

Rhiannon Cairns (9)	86
Liam Mackay (9)	86
Anna Whyte (9)	86
Louise Ann McDonald (9)	87
Kayleigh Murray (9)	87
Ronnie Anne Jarvie (9)	87
Ayeisha Mohammed (9)	88
Victoria Price (9)	88
Kirsty Lamb (8)	88
Michael Ian Caskie (8)	89
Lauren Gausden (9)	89
Ahsaan Razaq (8)	89
Luke Borthwick (8)	90
Tara Mahmood (9)	90
Matt Stephenson (9)	91
Zainab Rehman (8)	91
Christopher Neilson (9)	92
James Dawson (9)	92
Romaan Babar (9)	92
Aneesa Dastgir (9)	93
Storm Imrie (9)	93
Iona-Marie Callaghan (7)	93
Rose Ewins (7)	94
Stephanie Nixon (7)	94
Sean Imrie (8)	94
Taylor Hogg (7)	95

St Peter's Primary School, Edinburgh

Anya Vitaliev (8)	95
Mhairi-Claire McGowan (8)	95
Molly Keenan (8)	96
Neave Keenan (8)	96
Alessia Pasquariello (8)	96
Elissa Hasson (8)	97
Sinéad Millar (8)	97
Marcus Corrigan (8)	97
Matthew Laurie (8)	98
Mairi Mulvanny (8)	98
Eilidh Buchan (8)	98
Peter Blair (11)	99
Niamh Jarvis (9)	99

The Royal High Primary School

The Poems

The Playground In The Summer

I am standing in the playground
On a roasting hot day.
The sky is sparkling blue
And the burning sun is shining too.

The wonderful blue birds are singing
Our new summer tune.
The cheerful children
Are dancing madly.

The golden, crisp leaves
Are jumping back to their trees.
And the beautiful flowers
Are growing again.

The long, hot summer's day
Is sadly fading away.
As the sparkling blue sky
Turns into a dull grey, purple sky
We all wave goodbye and say goodnight.
Until the next summer day comes.

Lisa Kempton
Craigentinny Primary School

Glamour

Golden rings
Shine with beauty
Silver bracelets
Sparkle in the moonlight
Amazing outfits
Shimmers in the crowd
Gleaming jewellery
Glows in the night
The night of beauty
The night of glamour
The night it came back.

Gabi Twardowska (11)
Craigentinny Primary School

Sam And Her Ham

A girl called Sam
She ate lots of red raw ham
Then she became a clam.
With pink and white hair
She went everywhere
With her little pet bear.
Her mum did not know what to do
And she wore no clothes too!
She never turned up at school
Instead she went to a swimming pool.
Her friends were ashamed
And they got half the blame!
They went very mad
And did something bad.
I would tell you
But you would not like to know.

Heather Scott (12)
Craigentinny Primary School

I Am . . . My Mum

Fun maker
Family helper
Dinner cooker
Food shopper
Clothes buyer
Child collector
Good cuddler

I am . . . my mum.

Hubert Szer (8)
Craigentinny Primary School

What Did I See?

When I looked out of my window
What did I see?
I saw a dinosaur.
It was green and big.
His nails were long and grey.
His teeth were big and brown.
He has a purple bow tie.
His eyes were big and scary.
He wrecked the city.
He stole money.
He was so scary he growled.
Some people died not nice to know.
He destroyed lots of things.

Jamie Duffy (7)
Craigentinny Primary School

I Am . . . A Goldfish

Tail flapper
Goldfish colour
Big fins
Gold scales
Fat cheeks

I am . . . a goldfish.

Ewan Barclay (8)
Craigentinny Primary School

What Did I Feel?

When I looked out of my window,
What did I see?
A big fat monster staring at me!
He was fluffy.
He was blue.
He wears a hat.
He was spotty.
Was he friendly? Yes he was.
He said I will come and get you tomorrow.
The next day he picked me up . . .
And ate me.
In the monster tummy I squealed.
He spat me out and showed me around,
And then took me back to my room,
And now we are friends.

Andrew Pentony (7)
Craigentinny Primary School

I Am A Dog

Fast runner
Good hunter
Good jumper
Sneaky sniffer
Good racer
Ham eater
Good swimmer
Sharp teether

I am a dog.

Fiona Thomson (8)
Craigentinny Primary School

What Did I See?

When I looked out my window
What did I see?
A dragon standing outside my window.
He went into my door.
He had spikes on his back.
He has a big nose.
His feet are big, his hands are big.
He walks on two feet.
He is green everywhere.
But his feet were grey.
He went upstairs.
He went into my bedroom.
I hopped on his back.
A window in the roof went open.
We flew out.
We went on an adventure.
We went into his volcano.
There was treasure in his volcano.
Then we went home.

Celina Eisenhardt (7)
Craigentinny Primary School

I Am . . . A Polar Bear

Much colder
Always hungrier
Fish hunter
Keen killer
Loud roarer
Really whiter

I am . . . a polar bear.

Reece Hoskins (8)
Craigentinny Primary School

What Did I See?

I looked out my window
What did I see?
I saw a big monster looking at me.
He was playing with my soccer ball
He was hairy
He was funny
He was fat
He had two ears, one mouth and one eye
He said, My name is Mighty.'
He had a very funny voice that was like this; *shiii swash*
He wore no clothes
He never said much
We loved playing games.

Morgan McIntosh (7)
Craigentinny Primary School

What Did I See?

When I looked out of my window
What did I see?
A big fluffy monster looking at me.
She was pink with purple spots.
She had big brown eyes.
She had red spots on her nose
She had long brown hair with a red bow,
She is ten and she says,
'I am a good girl
I am, I am.'

Katie Ewart (7)
Craigentinny Primary School

My Monster

When I looked out my window
What did I see?
A big monster staring at me!
With slimy, dark, orange eyes.
Commits crimes too.
He was pink, fuzzy and had green hair at the top.
His tail flopped down like a mop.
And was pink all over.
His ears were red. I went back to bed.
He smashed my door open, crawled into my room.
There was a boom.
I opened my eyes.
He was lying on the floor.

Mehreen Zaman (7)
Craigentinny Primary School

I Am . . . A Tiger

Fast runner
Good jumper
Sneaky sniffer
Lazy sleeper
Good swimmer
Meat lover
Bad respecter
Good hunter

I am . . . a tiger.

Gina Tulloch (9)
Craigentinny Primary School

What Is . . . The Moon?

The moon is a silver football
Floating in a puddle.

It is white milk
Spilt on a black pavement.

It is white wool
Laying in a black basket.

It is a shining white balloon
Drifting in the dark night.

It is a pale white plate
Lying on a black tablecloth.

It's a white thumb print
Printed on a black piece of paper.

It is a silvery sequin
Dropped on a black road.

It is a sparkling white flare
Shooting in the dark night.

Sean McNicoll   (9)
Craigentinny Primary School

I Am . . . My Dog!

High jumper
Fast runner
Spider eater
Shoe biter
Upstairs leaper
Knocker overer
People tripper
Quick licker
Football player

I am . . . my dog!

Ryan Black   (8)
Craigentinny Primary School

What Did I See?

I looked out of my window
What did I see?
I saw a T-rex staring at me!
The T-rex is big and funny.
The T-rex is good at telling jokes.
The T-rex is a vegetarian.
The T-Rex is brown, black and green.
He is called Rexy.
He speaks like Hi, hi, hi,
Rexy has lots of friends.
His tail is big.
He loves custard.
He loves school.
He loves to play catch.
He is a good T-rex.
I love Rexy.

Ross Cootes (8)
Craigentinny Primary School

I Am . . . Me!

Lego builder
Xbox 360 player
Movie watcher
Golden time liker
Star Wars pretender

I am . . . me!

Joseph Daniels-Sitch (8)
Craigentinny Primary School

What Is The . . . Ocean?

The ocean is a frightening tiger
pouncing on its prey.

It is a tough robber
trying to smash a bank window.

It is a blue pen
swirling angrily on a freshly made piece of paper.

It is a turquoise dice
getting battered and bumped along the dining room table.

It is a blue paged dictionary
getting flicked from page to page on a school desk.

It is a beautiful butterfly
struggling for breath in a rippling bird bath.

It is a shining fish
undulating on sandy dry land.

It is an elegant gymnast
doing graceful rolls and swings on shining new apparatus.

It is a blue flower
swaying lightly in a small, calm breeze.

Keir Aitken (9)
Craigentinny Primary School

Darkness

Darkness is black like a dog.
It sounds like mad barking.
It tastes like rotten milk.
It smells like a pig.
It looks like fog.
It feels like smooth fur.
It reminds me of when I couldn't find the door handle.

Frazer Mack (8)
Craigentinny Primary School

What Are . . . The Stars?

The stars are glitter sprinkled on black paper
Shining their hearts out.

They are shining diamonds
Posing in the sky.

They are lots of chalk
Standing on a blackboard.

They are white seagulls
Flying in the deep night sky.

They are flickering candles
High in the sky.

They are dots of Blu-Tac
Sticking on a black wall.

They are sprinkles of shining sand
On a hard, black stone.

Cameron Shade (9)
Craigentinny Primary School

I Am . . . A Monkey

Dirty flyer
Tree climber
Good jumper
Banana lover
Fast runner
Long tailer
King climber
Filthy animal

I am . . . a monkey.

Lewis McKay (8)
Craigentinny Primary School

What Did I See?

Last night when I looked out my window
What did I see?
A big blue monster
With two heads and square eyes and fluffy ears.
I invited him to tea.
He was really funny!
I was smiling
The monster was fat as well
He was smelly.
The monster's name is Jack.
I took him home.
I said goodbye.
I was sad.

Aimee McInnes (7)
Craigentinny Primary School

I Am . . . A Fisherman

Boat sailor
Fish hooker
Hat wearer
Fish catcher
Crab eater
Fish nibbler
Salmon liker
Shark hater

I am . . . a fisherman.

David Lusted (8)
Craigentinny Primary School

What Did I see?

I looked out of my window
What did I see?
A really big snowman
Staring at me.

He liked playing football
The snowman can fly
He takes me with him
He eats carrots then he says
Yummy, yummy, in my tummy.

He looks like a fat person
And has a button nose
And two coal eyes
My snowman loves me.

Sean Hughes (7)
Craigentinny Primary School

I Am . . . Homer Simpson!

Fat bummer
Bald header
Silly manner
Noisy eater
Silly singer
Skinny legger
Weird rider
Cool motor

I am . . . Homer Simpson!

Jamie Murphy (8)
Craigentinny Primary School

The Little Fat Cat

My little fat cat
As black as a dark midnight sky
She plays in the small green garden
And fights any cat that goes by.

My little fat cat
Can be nicer than that
She can curl up next to the warm fireplace
And she will stick her small tongue out at me!

My little fat cat
Will do things like that
She is a sweet, little, cute angel
But she won't be nice if she spots
Sweet little mice
That's my little fat cat!

Samantha Paget (11)
Craigentinny Primary School

What Did I See?

One night a boy was sleeping.
He heard a noise.
His curtains started to move and . . . there was a monster.
He was hairy and green
He had three eyes and five noses,
Long dirty nails
He woke up.
'It's a dream,' he said.
And he never got scared.

Yusra Tawfiq (7)
Craigentinny Primary School

Glen Affric - The Green Mountain

Bright green trees
Crammed together
On the mountain.
The clear blue sky
Shines on navy water.
Seeing double
A beautiful place
Repeated.

Jack Roden (11)
Craigentinny Primary School

I Am . . . A Cat

Water hater
Mouse lover
Fish eater
Paw licker
Furry facer

I am . . . a cat.

Samantha Thomson (8)
Craigentinny Primary School

Undiscovered

Ripples in puddles of water
Left behind by the tide.
One hundred blurry buildings
Upside down.
Sections of sand lying undiscovered.

Christopher Smith (11)
Craigentinny Primary School

What Did I See?

When I looked out my window
I saw a dinosaur.
The dinosaur was a lambeosaur
It smiled at me.
I smiled back at it.
I saw the dinosaur come out of a big door.
It was tall.
It had blue eyes and a blue face.
A green neck too.
The dinosaur was good, it put me to bed.
It said goodnight.

Brandon Sives (8)
Craigentinny Primary School

I Am . . . A Shark

Blood smeller
Cool killer
Nice never
Always badder
Swims faster
Fishermen hater
Friendly never

I am . . . a shark.

Lucy Malone (8)
Craigentinny Primary School

My Cat Inky!

My frisky cat Inky
Likes to play with her mouse.
As she slips and she skids
On the floors in the house.

She's always very naughty
She always runs around our house.
As she plays and slides
Chasing after her toy mouse.

She is nearly three now
And she's still very frisky.
She's active and happy
That's my cat Inky.

Kim Paterson (11)
Craigentinny Primary School

What Did I Hear?

When I was in my bed I heard a hissing noise.
I went to the loo
I looked up the drainpipe
Ssss Ahhh
The boy said
'It is a hissy, hissy snake.'
It was green and brown
And had big eyes that were round
And it was hissing.
It was sticking its tongue out.
His tongue was red and it was stripy.

Kane O'Connor (7)
Craigentinny Primary School

What Are . . . The Stars?

The stars are glittering diamonds
Lying in a jewellery box.

They are shining glitter
Sprinkled on black paper.

They are silver sparkling sequins
Sparkling on black shoes.

They are gold earrings
Strewn on a black dressing table.

They are gold beads
Glittering on a black, long dress.

Sophie Ormiston (9)
Craigentinny Primary School

What Did I See?

When I looked out my window
What did I see?
I saw a snowman looking back at me.
He was green and pointy.
He had sharp teeth and had red blood hair.
He could speak French and English and he had a car.
He could eat a hundred people in one second.
He could transform into anything he wanted
And he can't melt.

Lewis Dalgleish (7)
Craigentinny Primary School

What Is The . . . Moon?

It is a white plate
Lying on a black table.

It is a large hubcap
For my car.

It is a big cake
With glittering cherries.

It is a giant Frisbee
Getting thrown up in the sky.

It is a silver, round clock
Ticking and tocking all day in a dark blue room.

Blair Garry Lee Young (10)
Craigentinny Primary School

If I Were A Butterfly

If I were a butterfly
I would dance in the air
To get people's attention.

I would go to dancing classes
So I could be a glorious dancer
When I grow up.

I would get wing dye
So I could get some brand new
Fantastic colours for my wings.

Casey Baillie (9)
Craigentinny Primary School

What Is . . . The Moon?

The moon is a golden clock
Ticking on a dark blue wall.

It is a white Frisbee
High in the dark blue sky.

It is a white dinner plate
Lying on a blue tablecloth.

It is a silver round tablecloth
Lying on a blue floor.

It is a shiny ball
Kicked up in the sky.

Callum Farrell (10)
Craigentinny Primary School

The Red T-Rex

When I looked out my window
I saw a T-Rex
It was red and big and scary
With big teeth.
He lived in a cave.
He had very sharp claws.

Natasha Kitt & Natasha Robinson (7)
Craigentinny Primary School

What Is A Rainbow?

A rainbow is multicoloured clothes
Hanging in a wardrobe.

It is colourful pencils
Standing on a table.

It is a multicoloured scarf
Lying on a bed in a bedroom.

It is colourful balloons
Floating in the sky.

Hannah Ross (9)
Craigentinny Primary School

What Did I See?

When I looked out my window
What did I see?
A big growling dinosaur staring at me.
It had big eyes and saliva coming from its mouth.
Big blue teeth and claws like bricks.
And hair like spikes.
I like my dinosaur.
He is good.

Connor Ross (8)
Craigentinny Primary School

I Am A Penguin

I'm adorable
I'm black and white
I catch fish
I dive in the water
I eat fish
I'm funny
I'm as good as gold
I have orange Mohican hair
I live in the South Pole
I jump
I clap
I lie on my back
I have a mama
I am naughty
I'm obvious to see
I peck
I roll
I slide
I'm tall
I swim under the water
I vandalise ice
I'm a winner
I'm extraordinary
I'm yummy
I live in the zoo.

Liam King (9)
Craigentinny Primary School

What Am I?

Fish eater
Fast simmer
Good diver
Amazing flipper
Brilliant tricker
Sea lover
Person liker
Cute babies
Good carer
Shark hater
Fun splasher.

Answer: a dolphin.

Kirsty Scott (9)
Craigentinny Primary School

Chainsaw

A bird hater
An egg breaker
A hand slicer
An animal runner
A nest faller
An ear hater
A voice breaker.

Michael Robertson (9)
Craigentinny Primary School

Stunning Ballet Dancers

Stunning ballet dancers
Jumping to the clouds
Footsteps tiptoeing
Floating across the floor

Stunning ballet dancers
Gliding like swans
Spinning like hurricanes
Flying through the air

Stunning ballet dancers
Children miming madly
Bouncing bunnies
Jumping to the clouds

Stunning ballet dancers
Happy and embarrassed
Dancing around
Curling very small

Stunning ballet dancers
Voices shouting instructions
And we run,
Jump,
Turn,
Balance,
And run

Stunning ballet dancers
Running like mice
Stretching out wide
As quiet as elephants
Stunning ballet dancers.

Katherine Thomson (10)
Craigentinny Primary School

Mmmmm

There is a
Way to make
Them sweet,
But you want,
More, after
More.
You spend
A fortune
Filling your
Pockets.
They taste delightful but
Too many make
You sick.
Some have sugar or sherbet
In them or
Over them.
They are all eaten
During the interval.

Jake Gordon (11)
Craigentinny Primary School

Loch Fyne

Shining on the loch,
A dark black castle.
Wiggly water moving slowly
Ducks gliding
Sky so bright, a shepherd's delight.

Jillian Denney (11)
Craigentinny Primary School

If I Were Bart Simpson

If I were Bart Simpson
I would sprint to school
Because I missed the bus and was late for school.
I would go on the skateboard with no clothes
Because Homer said so.
I would go on the horse and have races
And win the World Cup.
I would help Homer on the roof
To hammer his head.
I would play with Millhouse in the tree house
Whenever I was bored.

Aasim Afzal (9)
Craigentinny Primary School

My Doggy!

I am staring at a little pup,
He's blond, he's soft and has some spots,
He runs in the green garden,
Like a cat crazily chasing its prey,
He greedily eats his food,
Like a person on an extreme diet!
He carefully guards his bone,
Like a leprechaun with a pot of gold!
He is so smelly it's like inside a welly!

Hannah Shade (11)
Craigentinny Primary School

What Are The . . . Stars?

The stars are like silver diamonds
Glittering in the dark blue sky.

They are jewels
Lying on a dark blue table.

They are glittering stars
Glued on a black piece of paper.

They are glitter
Sparkling in the dark blue sky.

Caitlyn Black (9)
Craigentinny Primary School

Living Land

Golden fields
Hidden by trees.
Ruin upon a hill.
Quiet blue sky,
Lizards alive on the beach.
Sleepy summer
Dry boat upon white sand.
Joyful.

Rhys Hamilton (11)
Craigentinny Primary School

All Alone

Here I am standing all alone
Nothing to worry about and nothing to do
The fast wind in my cold face
Wondering what I should immediately do.

As the children run around me
Screaming, laughing and shouting
And me standing bored, just looking
Around the cold and frosty park.

I wonder what it's like to have friends
Playing, screaming and laughing with me
I just wish I had a nice friend
Just even one that would share her
Secrets and share her feelings with me.

Nor Tawfig
Craigentinny Primary School

What Is A . . . Rainbow?

A rainbow is colourful pencils laying down on a table.
It is big books standing up against a library book stand.
It is colourful lines drawn on a whiteboard.
It is flower petals growing in a garden.
It is clothes nice and tidily folded in a wardrobe.
It is a rainbow-coloured dress hanging on a coathanger.
It is a coloured bottle standing on a table.

Tiegan Patterson (9)
Craigentinny Primary School

Very Snowy Dog - Haiku

Oh the snowy day
All the sun has gone away
Oh what a good day.

Megan Ewart
Craigentinny Primary School

What Are . . . Stars?

The stars are glittering jewels
Zooming in the sky.

They are pieces of glitter
Glowing in the water.

They are silver coins
Falling from a blue table.

They are sparkling diamonds
Whizzing around black paper.

Tabatha Harrison (9)
Craigentinny Primary School

What Are The Stars?

The stars are like shiny diamonds
Glittering high in the sky.

They are like gold and silver glitter
Shining on a black piece of paper.

They are like shining jewels
Glittering in a shop window.

They are like a group of seagulls
Flying in the sky.

Erin Lawrence (9)
Craigentinny Primary School

What Is The Star?

The star is a shiny diamond glittering in the sky.
It is a piece of glitter swinging on a tree.
A silver plant on a blue table.
It is a silver piece of frost on a black bridge.

Michael Laidlaw (9)
Craigentinny Primary School

Gorilla

I am amazing
I am a banana lover
I climb
I am dangerous
I am energetic
I am furious
I am gigantic
I am hilarious
I am impossible
I have jaws
I kill
I'm lazy
I moan
I'm noisy
I am original
I am positive
I'm quiet
I respect
I am strong
I am mostly trouble.

Michal Twardowski (9)
Craigentinny Primary School

I Am A Dog

Woof! Woof!
Say the dogs
On a summery morning
With the sun shining bright.

Pant! Pant!
Say the dogs
Sitting outside
Enjoying the sun.

Jamie Ramsay (8)
Craigentinny Primary School

Gorilla

I attack amazingly.
I am black.
I climb trees.
I'm dangerous.
I eat fruit.
I frighten animals.
I growl.
I am hairy.

Justin Byars (9)
Craigentinny Primary School

Dog

I argue with dogs,
I bite people,
I'm cute to my family,
I dig up bones in the garden,
I eat loads of food,
I have fun,
I am gorgeous.

What am I . . .?

Tiegan Brown (9)
Craigentinny Primary School

What Am I?

Deep sleeper
Fast runner
Good footballer
Good friend
Great drawer
Funny laugher

Answer: my friend Sophie.

Katelyn Lothian (9)
Craigentinny Primary School

Zebra

I am amazing
I am bad at scaring people
I am skilled at confusing people
I'm a dazzling sight
I am an energetic runner
I am a brilliant finder
I am a good runner
I am a happy hopper
I am a . . .

Emma Robertson (9)
Craigentinny Primary School

Linlithgow Loch

Big, white, fluffy clouds
Above big rocky mountains
A small home hidden by tall trees
Flowing water under a bridge far away
Beautiful warm autumn colours.

Martyna Szer (10)
Craigentinny Primary School

I Am A Hamster

I am a hamster
I am attractive
I bring love
I love climbing
I do lots of climbing
I eat lots
I am fast.

Dylan McCardle (9)
Craigentinny Primary School

Puppy

A feet licker
A panting maker
A tail wagger
A big sniffer
A loud barker
A serious growler
I am a . . .

Megan Jeffrey (9)
Craigentinny Primary School

My Dog Zeus - Haiku

My dog is called Zeus
He is a black Rottweiler
He's too strong for me!

Rhys Sinclair
Craigentinny Primary School

Navy

A great shouter
A noise maker
A hat wearer
A world traveller
Put these together
I am in the . . .

Gage Grant (9)
Craigentinny Primary School

Kennings

Good looker
Visits the hairdresser
Fast runner
Nice charmer
Loud and noisier
Wonderful smiler
Amazing sporter
Great footballer
Fabulous outfitter
Fantastic basketballer

I'm . . . Clark.

Laura McGovern (8)
Craigentinny Primary School

Puppies

I am adorable,
I am a good barker,
I am cute,
I am disagreeable,
I am energetic,
I am funny to watch,
I am the greatest animal,
I am helpful in lots of ways,
I am a . . . puppy!

Zara Burgess (9)
Craigentinny Primary School

Kennings

Gorgeous facer
Always smarter
Marvellous girler
Proper pester
Great talker
Fast walker
Great smiler
Good joker

I am . . . Laura.

Clark O'Connor (8)
Craigentinny Primary School

Puppy

I'm amazing at tricks,
I bite you,
I'm cute to people,
I dig soil,
I eat lots of food,
I'm fantastic at chasing,
I'm gorgeous,
What am I?

Rachael Cook (9)
Craigentinny Primary School

The Fish And The Fish Tank

Splash, splash
Goes the fish in the
Fish tank while it zooms
Wiggles going to get food. His
Fins are lost in scales. Bubble, bubble
Thud, thud went the fish banging on the
Glass. The fish was trying to get in the dish.
Tap, tap as the girl touched the bowl. Bang
Bang the girl sang. She shook the bowl. It fell
On the poor soul. Bang, bang, tap, tap,
Thud, thud, bubble, bubble
Splash, splash
Went the fish and
The fish tank smashed!

Kelsey Jane Hogg (10)
Craigentinny Primary School

Sharks

Man-eating sharks on their way
Hunting down for their prey
Powerful snapping jaws
Snap! Snap!
Huge nasty powerful killers
Man-eating sharks on their way
Eating and killing is all hard work for the day
Snap! Snap!
Snapping jaws empty stomachs and lips licked
Hey
Watch out
Gobble, gobble
Yum, yum.

Cody Stoddart (10)
Craigentinny Primary School

Slugs Are Horrible!

Horrible, horrible!
Slugs they are,
Slimy small
Horrible, horrible!
Slugs they are,
Slow not fast
They never last
Horrible, horrible
Slugs they are
If you see a slug,
Chuck it down the plug
Pop!
Horrible, horrible
Slugs they are . . .
Appalling!

Megan Kempton (10)
Craigentinny Primary School

Ballet Is Not My Thing!

Ballet is not my thing
I'd rather buy *bling-bling*
Sometimes it can be fun
Sometimes we tiptoe while we run
But that's not the way to solve ballet
As we tap our toes
Some people fall on their nose
While a butterfly comes out of a cocoon
Twisting by the sunset moon
Ballet is not my thing
I'd rather buy *bling-bling*
All trying to be as graceful as a swan
Trying not to make a thump
Still ballet is not my thing
I'd rather buy *bling-bling*.

Becky Crooks (10)
Craigentinny Primary School

Pigs

Oink, oink!
Pink, black and yellow
Cute little pigs are treated as shadows
They're taken away for your breakfast
Sausage, bacon and even ham
Now I know why they can't stay calm
Look in their eyes and you will see
These smart animals are not to be
Go to a farm on a hot summer's day
Splosh
And you will need a wash.

Catherine Rose (10)
Craigentinny Primary School

Snake

Slithery snake
Slyly moving down the road
Sliding on its slithery scales.

Its tongue darting out to find where it's going.
Kills small animals such as mice and insects.

Ewan Lennie (10)
Craigentinny Primary School

The Sun

The sun is a gigantic water balloon up in the sky.
If it bursts then water will go everywhere.

It is a clock ticking on the wall.

It is a gold coin on the ground.

It is a flower stuck into the ground.

Gerard Smillie (10)
Craigentinny Primary School

I Am A Shark

Good eater
Great water breaker
Sharp teeth
Excellent swimmer
Fish eater
Not friendly
Good biting skills.

Kyle Black (9)
Craigentinny Primary School

Me

Pizza lover
Good writer
Computer lover
Great dancer
Cat player
Fantastic speller.

Kerry McDonald (9)
Craigentinny Primary School

Monkeys

I am an athletic animal
I can do brilliant tricks
I am a good swinger
And you can see me in the zoo.

Alexander Ferguson (8)
Craigentinny Primary School

If I Were A Pen

If I were a pen
I would write the most famous stories and become
a best-selling author.
I would draw the most amazing pictures so they could get put
in the art gallery.
I would mark people's work to make people happy
I would write a letter to a child to tell the parent they were injured.

Chloe Hunter (9)
Craigentinny Primary School

Autumn Gardens

Beneath the cold and dark rocks,
An extremely slimy slug,
Slithering about trying to find food.

Above the trees,
A beautiful butterfly,
Was flying in the air.

Under a pile of leaves,
A spiky, brown hedgehog,
Lay in a rough ball.

On a juicy, green leaf,
A tiny spider,
Was spinning a lovely white web.

Katie O'Rourke (7)
Echline Primary School

Summer Garden

On a beautiful daffodil,
A big busy bee,
Is collecting yellow pollen.

Under a tree,
Lots of beetles,
Thinking lovely thoughts.

On a brown tree,
A caterpillar slithers,
Eating a small leaf.

Behind brown compost,
Medium hedgehogs,
Are in squishy mud.

Hamish Robinson (7)
Echline Primary School

Winter Gardens

Under the frozen pond
A beautiful fish
Trying to get to the food.

In the thick snow
A frozen red squirrel
Holding a nut as hard as a brick.

Sliding on the slippery ice
A big orange fox
Trying to get to the other side.

Inside a giant snowman
A family of hedgehogs
All cuddling to keep warm.

David MacNeill (7)
Echline Primary School

Summer Gardens

In a dark, but warm corner,
A purplish black spider,
Was spinning a shining web.

On a huge oak tree,
A red squirrel,
Was trying to find some nuts.

Wrapped in a cocoon,
A green caterpillar,
Was trying to turn into a butterfly.

On an evergreen tree,
A black crow,
Tried to steal some corn.

Lucy Guthrie (7)
Echline Primary School

Anger

Anger is red like hot chilli peppers,
It sounds like a wave from the sea,
It feels like I am burning myself on a fire,
It reminds me of a plane taking off,
It looks like a big and freaky vampire,
It smells like my dad's dinner,
It tastes like a strong mint.

Catherine Kelly (7)
Echline Primary School

Summer Gardens

Way above in the air.
Was an extremely beautiful butterfly
Floating gorgeously over the trees

Under the very, very dark ground
Was a disgusting worm
Discovering the world.

On the green flower
Was a buzzing bumblebee
Taking yummy pollen

Over the green hill
Was a spotty ladybird
Climbing the brown tree

Up on a long branch
Was a very slow snail
Eating munchy leaves for its tea.

Amy Rankin (7)
Echline Primary School

Autumn Gardens

In the white plant
A black spider
Spinning a big web.

Inside the black mud
A big slimy worm
Making a hole.

On a pink flower
A big stripy bee
Was flapping his wings.

Samantha Millar (7)
Echline Primary School

Spring Gardens

Beside a plank of dirty wood
A slimy woodlouse
Crawled creepily into a dark hedge.

Inside a dark pond
An old goldfish
Trying to find some tasty food.

On a huge stone
A green frog
Hopped on top of a bush.

Under a big black pebble
A slimy worm
Churning up lots of mud.

Hannah Baillie (7)
Echline Primary School

Anger

Anger is red like a firework exploding.
It sounds like a loud bark from a dog.
It feels like the chilli in my mouth.
It reminds me of a tiger.
It looks like a big angry mummy.
It smells like a burning tomato.
It tastes like a very spicy mint.

Chloë Sutherland (7)
Echline Primary School

Autumn Gardens

Over a tall wall
A family of buzzy
Bees dream to move house.

Michelle Peden (7)
Echline Primary School

Acrostic Poem

R ising rainbow
A mazing rainbow
I ncredible rainbow
N atural rainbow
B eautiful rainbow
O ver the rainbow
W et rainbow.

James Ferguson (7)
Echline Primary School

Art!

Art is smart,
Art is fun,
Art is colourful,
Art is messy,
Landscapes are art,
Painting is art,
Drawing is art,
Creativity is art,
Art is cool,
Art is amazing,
Art is enjoyable,
Art is great,
Yes! Art is smart.

Peter Robertson (9)
Flora Stevenson Primary School

Death

Me and my friends need help very soon
Blood and mud cover our skin; the life has been beaten out of us
Coughing up blood, hardly breathing
Our friendship is bonded by suffering and war
We have been here too long, we don't feel pain
It's just numb everywhere on our body
This is how dying feels but we haven't given up
Death is close though, very close
I taste fatal poison flowing inside me and I croak the word 'Gas'
I sense slow clumsy movement around me
Our gas masks are on us, we should be safe
Except him . . . blind, deaf and screaming
Green, black, blue I don't know which. My brain is closing down
I flail about trying to find my friend
Then I see him all screwed up inside and out
Now I realise that he is really dying
I'm holding him, he's cold, lifeless gasping for breath
I whisper to him a prayer as he takes his last breath
You don't understand, you can't imagine . . . Can you?
A dead man resting in my arms
The sounds are depressing almost unbearable
Nothing you've ever heard can match this
Coughing, rolling about lifeless, and dripping of blood
Maybe you feel nothing but I hope you have
Experienced what we felt on that day
Suffering endlessly for our country
How it felt to die.

Eilidh Cameron (11)
Flora Stevenson Primary School

The Northern Lights

The Aurora is a graceful dragon
Hanging in the Arctic skies
Floating amongst the stars
Draping the heavens with curtains of light
Glowing against the black velvet of night
Like finest gossamer.

Mint-green, rose-pink, ice-blue, blood-crimson
Trembling in the moonlight
Reflecting off ice
Soaring like a comet
Scattering stars
Like a cat among mice.

Weaving through starbeams
Spiralling around the sky
Flowing, wafting
Drifting in a celestial dance
For eternities.

Varshini Vijayakumar (11)
Flora Stevenson Primary School

House Fire

The fiery flares dance around the room
A burning dragon raining flames like a monsoon
It's fiery breath so warm and hot.

The clashing teeth and jaws are fierce,
A steel bridge, it could probably pierce.
No mercy the dragon shows,
All day the dragon wails its frightening roars.

The helpless humans try to escape,
The flames meet them, it's too late.

In the flames the dragon devours,
The whole house with its treacherous powers.

Umar Majid (11)
Flora Stevenson Primary School

Black

Black, the bewitching colour
I lie in bed,
Thoughts whizzing round my head,
I watch the darkness fill the sky,
(Like the sun saying, goodbye.)
A shadowy hand clasps my mouth,
I cannot scream, I cannot shout,
Darkness saunters round the room,
In some transfixing dance,
The moonlight shines through the window,
But still the room remains black,
Black shadows take over the bright orange walls of my bedroom,
Into a shadowy grey,
But black will go in the morning,
It's never here to stay,
Black, the colour of darkness.

Harriet Johnston (10)
Flora Stevenson Primary School

My Special Place

There is a special place I like to go
It's the place I feel safe and I call home
And every time that life goes bad
It is the place I don't feel sad.

It's my special place
Only I know of it
If it were real, it would mean a lot to me
But it's a dream only I can see
That makes it more special for me
It is my special place to be.

Jennifer Kerr (11)
Flora Stevenson Primary School

Simply Red

I see a river of red,
From all the blood shed.
My family and loved ones are gone,
That's when I realise I'm on my own.
I see the bodies scattered across the land,
I find my sibling and take hold of his hand.
He is lying next to the cherry tree,
We used to dance around when we were wee.
I remember what it used to look like,
But then the enemies had to strike.
I remember the strawberry field,
That has now been killed.
The apple tree, that once was free.
I see this city is dead,
Simply Red.

Fiona Begg (10)
Flora Stevenson Primary School

If I Ever Went To Space

If I should ever go to space
I'd look down on the human race
I'd try to solve all their fears
And stop the people shedding tears.

And if I ever went to Mars
I would look out to the stars
And wonder if there was anythin'
That I could call an alien.

Sean Carson (9)
Flora Stevenson Primary School

Holocaust Poem

Bashing the door, bashing, bashing louder and louder.
My mother screaming, father too,
Passing through the streets, rubble everywhere,
So much death and despair.
In the camps, death and starvation,
Do we deserve this despair,
Why do we have to bear this despair,
Just because we are Jews!
I am so depressed like a withering flower,
I just want to hold my mother and father,
Again just for an hour,
And here we are at the camp,
There's blood, there is death.
They bully us, they bully us,
They bully us to the bone,
This cannot be our final destination,
There are so many people against us
Just like one nation.

Katherine Allan & Ione Drummond (11)
Juniper Green Primary School

Sadness

Those horrible Germans murdering the Jews
Those poor Jews getting gassed and starved
Painful marching and there is no pity
Forcing them away from the city
People don't grow
Because their spirits are low
Not a smile not even a letter
Nothing ever gets better
Families don't get to be together
Because of the smoke you can't see the good weather.
Those horrible Germans murdering the Jews.

Sarah Dunn & Lauren McCabe
Juniper Green Primary School

Devastation For The Jews

Devastation in the camp,
Everything is bloody and damp,
Mass hatred massacre and blood,
Mothers screaming for their children,
They are nowhere to be found,
Toxic, terror and horrified people,
Sad, destruction and putrid smell,
Starving people on the ground,
The camp is filled by the screaming sound,
Gas chambers wield their wrath,
A day in the life of a Jew!

Fintan Purcell & Alistair Gordon (11)
Juniper Green Primary School

Holocaust Poem

The Jews were scared.
The Jews were hungry.
The Jews were beaten.
The Jews felt terrible.
The Jews were treated badly.
The Jews were tired.
The Jews were gassed!
The Nazis were cruel.
The Nazis were wrong.
The killing was pointless.
It was like living in Hell!

Evan Richards & Connor Ratcliffe (11)
Juniper Green Primary School

I Am A Jew

Crammed in a small space
Men with guns shouting, yelling
Marched at gun point
Is this what I get for being a Jew
People are starving, rotting away
I see a man, lying on the floor
The ground is no place for a bed
No wait, he's dead!
Is this what he gets for being a Jew?

We're in the depths of the camp now,
Away from our homes
I see more people
Skin and bones
Is this what they get for being a Jew?
We're loaded off a truck
And into a queue
I'm covered in muck
I smell bad too
Is this what I get for being a Jew?

We see burning bodies as we walk the path
They were all caught in the Nazi's wrath
Some of them butchered in half
Is that what they get for being a Jew?
We enter a chamber smelly but new
We're getting a shower
I need one too
I glance at the shower, as my life is about to pass
No wait, what's this? Gas!
I'm a Jew
What have I done to you?

Murray Drummond & Victor Pilard (11)
Juniper Green Primary School

Holocaust Poem

Chuck, chuck goes the train,
The Jews were kidnapped then were killed
All for being Jewish.
6 million died all for a nation's pride
There were funerals but no birthdays
A piece of bread and poisoned water
All for being a Jew
They cried for help but nobody came.
The sound of screams and bangs!
They were beaten up by big, bold bullies
All for being a Jew
The evil bullies of the Germans
They were tricked to go in the gas chambers
All for being a Jew
The betrayal of the Germans
All for being a Jew
There were nasty nights when no one was happy
Torture and cruel
All for being a Jew
The sick feeling of the dead
The gas chamber is the final torture
There is blood, there is death
All for being a Jew.

Fahad Iqbal & Andrew McNicoll (11)
Juniper Green Primary School

Holocaust Poem

Death is nearing,
By killer gas and hunger,
They are going to camp,
Herded like cows down the street,
They cry and cry,
Just skin and bones,
Every minute, people are dying,
Closer to camp, closer to death,
Hitler is evil, the Jews will die,
Unhappiness and desperation,
Soon they will come to the end of the tunnel,
Goodbye poor Jews, goodbye.

Phillipa Lumsden & Matthew Miller (11)
Juniper Green Primary School

White

All the snow is lying
It's so cold the babies are crying.
All the water is turning to ice
Seeing the children throwing snowballs is so nice.
It's so cold and so chilly
My cool snowman looks like Uncle Billy
The snow is falling so gently
The wind is roaring like the engine from a Bentley.

Cristiano Celini (12)
Craig Claperton (11) & Sandy
St Cuthbert's RC Primary School, Edinburgh

White Winter

White winter, outside today,
Prancing and dancing out on a sleigh,
Silently, snow falls on the ground,
While children, they play, running around
While snow falls, sleighs fall down the hills,
Children are saying, 'Mum take a chill pill.'
Chilly, icy, snow storms blow,
Santa's visiting soon, 'Ho, ho, ho!'
Kids are excited, what presents will they get?
While parents run around, getting really, really stressed,
It's getting late, time for tea,
What's for pudding? 'Wait and see,'
Santa's coming, time for bed,
We need to rest, our lazy heads,
It's midnight now, Santa's here,
We've given him a nice pint of beer.

Allannah Glanville
St Cuthbert's RC Primary School, Edinburgh

Snowy Day

Children clapping, adults laughing,
At the snowman made from ice.
Snowball fights everywhere.
Snowflakes drop from the sky,
Like little frozen leaves.

The crowded town, covered in white.
Children sliding on the sledges down the snowy hills.
Mums putting hats and gloves on, and dads throwing
Snowballs at each other.

Catherine Gunaseelan
St Cuthbert's RC Primary School, Edinburgh

White As Snow

Children laughing, parents clapping,
At a man made from white ice;
Snowflakes drop from the sky,
Like little leaves from the white trees;
Frozen streets fill the city,
Kids walking with smiles on their faces;
People sliding on their sledges,
Down the snowy hills;
Mums putting on hats and gloves,
Dads throwing snowballs;
All having fun in something
White as snow.

Antonella Carpico (11)
St Cuthbert's RC Primary School, Edinburgh

White Snow

The white snow starts to lie.
All the birds start to fly.
The snow is making white walls.
It's starting to freeze waterfalls.
Super sledging down the hill,
The snow starts to rest on the window sill.
The super snow is melting now
All the cows are happy now.
The snow has gone for another year.
The men are cheering with some beer.

Conor McGarrity & Danny Dallas (11)
St Cuthbert's RC Primary School, Edinburgh

A Black Bundle

A blind bundle
A small tumble

A toy chaser
A play maker

A ball player
A time waster

A tail shaker
A black bouncer

A sleep sleeper
A grey head.

Have you guessed it's a dog?

Laurie Canning (11)
St Cuthbert's RC Primary School, Edinburgh

A Pink Bundle

A pink bundle
A slimy flop

A fast grower
A fun player

A fluffy friend
A boisterous girl

A slow walker
An old learner

A recipe to make me a dog!

Shanice Silbourne (11)
St Cuthbert's RC Primary School, Edinburgh

Grumpy Sky

Watching the grey teary clouds go by
With their grumpy expressions
The sky with no colour
Like the 60's television
No sign of life
Just grumpy clouds
Floating by steamy windows
Lying in my bed
Listening to the sky growl
Like an angry dog
I dream about the sunny day
I feel I'll never see.

Olivia Hand
St Cuthbert's RC Primary School, Edinburgh

Christmas Thank Yous

Dear Mum and Dad
Thank you for the mobile phone
It will really come in handy
You will be glad to know I'll no longer moan
About not having a phone.

Niamh Quigley (10)
St Cuthbert's RC Primary School, Edinburgh

The Old Sponge In The Tub

There was an old sponge
In a tub it came out to play
And went away that day.
The old sponge in the tub.

Amber Alexandra Robertson (11)
St Cuthbert's RC Primary School, Edinburgh

The Rush Hour Bus

When I got on the 23
That was just the start for me.
Hot and smelly yes it was.
But no one knew what was the cause.
Toddlers fussing,
Babies crying,
Mothers hushing,
Grandma's sighing,
No one knew what was the cause,
But I think I know,
Who it was.
Business men pushing past,
Builders' bums, I was aghast,
Selfish people sitting down,
I looked at them with a frown,
These are just my thoughts and views.
On the buses and the queues,
Off the bus, home at last,
The rush hour bus goes whizzing past.

Hannah Foster (11)
St Mary's Music School, Edinburgh

The Nightmare Bridge

The area around is covered with mist
The suspension is golden and never snaps
It goes on and on and underneath
No river lies but nightmares and bad dreams
For this is a bridge to the dream world
Warning: Don't fall off
Nightmares lie ahead!

Duncan Robertson (10)
St Mary's Music School, Edinburgh

Time To Go To Angelo

To Chris I said, 'I'm on my way,
To little Angelo.
That special, pretty, little place,
That many people know.'

'In Angelo shmonkeys purrr,
And luns are made of jelly.
The seven-headed squilabongs
Each wear a spotty welly.'

'I'm going to climb a thousand stairs,
That look like giant snakes.
They hiss and twist and hiss some more,
Their eyes like shining lakes.'

'I'm prepared to dodge a giant bee,
A purple stinging one.
It's 10 foot 3, 3 times of me
And weighs 800 tonnes.'

'I'm ready to cross a wobbly bridge,
That's made of elastic bands,
Underneath is boiling lava,
And beside it is the land.'

'And finally, I'll get to there,
After 50 days.
With all the beautiful beaches,
The coastlines and the bays.'

'I'm going now, I'm on my way,
I'm too tired, I think I'll stay.'

Rowan Haslam (11)
St Mary's Music School, Edinburgh

The Forest Of Dreams

Life is one confusing metaphor
Nothing is really how it seems
It's freezing cold - snowflakes fall
But they're sweltering sunbeams!

Monkeys swing among the trees
Making trumpeting noises
Or could they be elephants?
There are so many choices!

My new eyes are staring
At a magical new world
And new strange animals creep
Around each bend and curl!

This is a picture of imagination
For it all just seems too real
My mind is spinning wildly
On an ever frantic wheel.

Mountains form in the distance
Clouded by a fog
Of ancient smoke from houses
Long buried in a muddy bog.

I really don't like living
In a world so immature
Is this just a nightmare
Or could it be the future?

Sally Carr (11)
St Mary's Music School, Edinburgh

Wishes

Wishes are powerful,
Wishes are great,
They will come unsuspected,
But never too late.

They will shine so brightly,
Or glide through the sky,
Walk right beside you,
Stay when you die.

Nobody knows, really,
If you're right or wrong,
The time is not exact,
For the taking's so long.

So keep them carefully,
Don't keep them too near,
For one day if you're lucky,
They might reappear.

Lydia Upton (11)
St Mary's Music School, Edinburgh

Be Mine

If you won't be mine,
It will be depressing.
You'd make my heart shine,
Oh no I'm already stressing.
You're running out of time,
Just be my valentine!

Isla Short (11)
St Mary's Music School, Edinburgh

A Poem About Feelings

I'm as happy as a snake with a rat.
I'm as happy as a cat in bed.
I'm as lonely as a dog in a cage.
I'm as sad as a monkey without its banana.
I'm as unhappy as a lion that's lost its meat.
I'm as happy as a dragon when it eats people.
I'm as sad as an ant when it gets stood on.
I'm as lonely as a butterfly when it's alone.

Jamie Leadbetter (9)
St Mary's Primary School, Bonnyrigg

Happy

Happy is yellow like beautiful daffodils in the spring.
Happy sounds like birds singing in a tree.
Happy looks like the sun shining bright far in the sky.
Happy smells like my mum's favourite perfume.
Happy tastes like chocolate dripping off the top of a cone.
Happy feels like your cuddly teddy in your bed.

Kelly-Anne Fairbairn (9)
St Mary's Primary School, Bonnyrigg

Upset

Upset is pale like tears dripping down your face.
Upset sounds like people laughing at you.
Upset looks like a stream of tears.
Upset smells like bitter grey smoke.
Upset tastes like saltwater from the sea.
Upset feels like being away from my mum while I am at school.

Jodi Herron (9)
St Mary's Primary School, Bonnyrigg

The Titanic Lives On

I could see it
It was lying there doing nothing
The big black boat lying there like an oily whale on its side.

I could see it
The golden funnels gone as rusty as a chain on my bike
The dooming dark, dull boat was an old piece of junk
Why was it so important?

I could see it
The round windows all cracked
And all the furniture broken.

I could see it
The propellers all worn out
And the squeaking of it still falling apart.

I could see it
The captain's bony body lying on the sandy seabed
With his hat still on.

From that moment I realised
Titanic lives on.

Taylor Garman (11)
St Mary's Primary School, Bonnyrigg

Horrified

Horrified is black like the lights going out when you're all alone.
Horrified is scary like a witch casting a spell over her children.
Horrified is screaming like lasers coming closer
And you've nowhere else to run.
Horrified is poisonous like poison running down the back of your throat.
Horrified is sickening like sour lemons that are out of date.
Horrified is bony like a dead rat's skeleton.

Abbie Gallacher (9)
St Mary's Primary School, Bonnyrigg

Anger

Anger is red like the flames of the Devil at the centre of Hell.
Anger is gooey like a load of slime falling on your head.
Anger is jaggy like prickly thorns touching your face.
Anger is bitter like poison going down your throat.
Anger is loud like a wolf howling at the dead of night.
Anger is furious like the sea on a stormy day.

James Ross (9)
St Mary's Primary School, Bonnyrigg

Frightened

Frightened is black like the night sky on a cold winter's night.
Frightened sounds like a wolf howling under the light of the moon.
Frightened looks like a spooky tunnel, knowing you have
                                          to go through it.
Frightened smells like my brother's old football shoes.
Frightened tastes like a sour lemon just been picked.
Frightened feels like horrible slime just came out of a freezer.

Becca Shields (9)
St Mary's Primary School, Bonnyrigg

White Winter

On a windy winter night the sparkly snow was landing.
The frozen ferrets were squawking on the tops of the trees.
The white water was melting all around.
The frozen flowers were like icy ice cubes.
The winter wonderland was pure white and icy.
The frozen farm was cold and damp.
The soft snow was going all slushy.
The frosty forest was getting dark.

Alicia Boniface (10)
St Ninian's RC Primary School, Livingston

White Christmas

Away we go ho, ho, ho
Santa's reindeer fly away
Sparkling snow falls down from the sky.
Frozen trees with no leaves,
Christmas cut in half with delicious jam inside.
Ripe robbers robbing the bank in a winter wonderland.
A little baby in her pram holding her blanket of snow.
Icy icicles under my nose
Frozen ferrets hibernating in their homes.
I use my sledge on the slippery ice going down the hill
Then I hurt my head.
Farmfoods sell their turkey and pudding for later.
When I wake up on that Christmas morning
I bolt downstairs,
Open my presents
But my favourite part is Christmas dinner.
My turkey leg in my mouth and sausages wrapped in bacon
And mash and tomato sauce.
Then get my pudding covered in cream.
It's time to go to bed.
Can't wait until next year.

James McFaul (10)
St Ninian's RC Primary School, Livingston

Winter Day

In winter wonderland's frozen farms in the countryside frozen flowers
and white weeds,
Slippery snow on the ground people were laughing
on their snow sledges.
Blankets of snow covered the trees and the grass, sparkly snow
on the rooftops.

People go nuts for the snow.

Reece McLaughlin (10)
St Ninian's RC Primary School, Livingston

Winter Snow

Winter snow frozen cold crystal ice shining bright very slowly snow falls,
The old cold tree shivers while snow falls off its branches,
Silver snow sparkling
When you wake up then you hear school is cancelled.
You run outside with your welly boots on, having fun friends
                                        come over to play.
Snow starts to melt when the sun shines down.
Boys and girls go back inside moping and groaning
                                    because the snow is gone
But now there's only ice to slide on before it turns to water.
Children will cheer when the snow comes back for now that's the end.
Until snow comes again, happy snow year.

Bethan Frew (10)
St Ninian's RC Primary School, Livingston

Children Playing In The Snow

One cold, frosty winter's day the wind was whistling
And the snow was falling onto the ground
Boys and girls were sledging and making snowmen
Every time it snows the kids are always out playing and having fun
But when it becomes too cold their mums always tell them to come in
They moan and groan, if they could they would stay out forever
They hate coming in, it spoils their fun.

Cameron McCue (10)
St Ninian's RC Primary School, Livingston

Winter Wonderland

Frozen ferrets scatter across the snow,
Children building icy igloos with frozen fingers,
Mam's making Christmas cake,
Silvery streams frozen by the cold
Winter weeds frozen to a block,
White mountains in the background of the sky,
Red robins flying up high,
Singing sparrows pecking at the earth
Dotty dogs slipping on the ice,
Tottering trees white with snow,
Happy hedgehogs hibernating in the ground,
Toddlers throwing heaps of snow,
Sledges sliding down the hill,
Parents drinking eggnog
Let's hope Santa comes.

Daniel Steele (10)
St Ninian's RC Primary School, Livingston

Wintry

One day, one wintry day
Everything turns all white.
Winter weeds turn wintry,
The water is so clear,
If you look in, it's clear as white water.
People are in cooking and cleaning,
Some people bake Christmas cakes.
People play silver sledges
And make wintry wonder.
Frosty farms and frosty fruit
Feast so bad. The fun it
Gives us and bad fevers.

Sohaib Ajaz (10)
St Ninian's RC Primary School, Livingston

Winter

The frozen breeze blows.
While the sky gently snows.
Dark and icy,
Icy and dark,
Wait till you see the perishing park.
Slippery streets,
Icy cold park seats.
A mist of steam,
The moon glows like a beam.
Then the sun rises.
And that is a signal for the snow,
To go.

Michael Keenan (10)
St Ninian's RC Primary School, Livingston

A Winter Poem

The white lovely snow
Surrounded around me
Icy icicles hanging from the houses
Frosty paths, slippery on the road.
Children playing on their sledges
Rest are snuggled in bed
Flowers are frozen, waiting for spring
So are we waiting patiently
There is snow everywhere
It's into a winter wonderland.

Ryan Lithgow (10)
St Ninian's RC Primary School, Livingston

Winter Is Here

The friends go through the frozen forest
Silver snow makes the snowman
They now go home for Christmas cake
Christmas cake isn't in a can
Frozen food and fun Christmas is not a fake
Winter wonderland wonderful for everyone
The white water turns to icy ice
Christmas pudding we love some
None stay in on a snowy day so nice
South fly the birds
Snowy sledge slides down the hill
Today banana and chocolate curd
We won't fall down like Jack and Jill.

Brandon Turner (10)
St Ninian's RC Primary School, Livingston

The Winter Feeling

Over the ground lies a mantel of white
A Heaven of diamonds shine down through the night.
Two hearts are thrilling,
In spite of the chilling,
Together

Love knows no season
Love knows no gloom,
Romance can blossom in any old tune.
Here in the open,
We're hopping and popping
Together.

Thomas McKeon (10)
St Ninian's RC Primary School, Livingston

Winter

Frozen footballs are flying in the air.
I am glad I've got hair
The silver stream flows
While my hair blows in the wind.
I am playing in a blanket of snow.
My cheeks are aglow.
My gran is making Christmas cake.
My gran is now making a tuna bake.
Then she goes back to the cake,
Children try to build icy igloos.
Then they go back home to bed.
Waiting for snowy Santa.
Ho! Ho! Ho!
Santa's coming.

Emily Daly (10)
St Ninian's RC Primary School, Livingston

White Snow

Here we go in the snow
The white, white snow
Frozen farms, frozen flowers
Frozen frost with snow on top
Going down the hill with
My new sledge
Goes over the hedge oh no my sledge
Christmas cake, ready for
Santa or the reindeers
Rudolph ready for take off
Dinner, steak, steak, steak pie.

Del Imrie (10)
St Ninian's RC Primary School, Livingston

Scotland

S cottish thistles are pretty.
C rowded cities are hard to get through.
O utside is nice but very cold.
T atties are good with haggis.
L och Ness hides a deadly monster.
A nd I like Edinburgh Museum.
N essie lives in Loch Ness.
D o you want to come and stay?

John Heaney (8)
St Ninian's RC Primary School, Livingston

Scotland

S kye has stormy seas
C astles in the crowded city
O ceans are very stormy
T rees are very green
L and is small
A urora Borealis is a beautiful sight
N essie is so beautiful
D o you like Scotland?

Kerri Mackay (9)
St Ninian's RC Primary School, Livingston

Red . . .

Red is a rose that sprung in spring.
Red is a loving heart.
Red is blood running through my veins.
Red is my puppy dog's collar.
Red is a pretty dress
Red is leaves in autumn.
Red is a fiery volcano.

Karina Carroll (8)
St Ninian's RC Primary School, Livingston

Red Is . . .

Red is the lava on Mustafar.
Red is the lightsaber of Darth Vader.
Red is the blast of a gun in a war.
Red is the colour of blood from a clone.
Red is the colour of evil,
Red is the sign of doom,
Red is the colour of Queen of Naboo's robe.

Elliott Young (9)
St Ninian's RC Primary School, Livingston

Lollipop

Lollipop, lollipop you're sugar and spice
And all things nice.
Sugar, sweet, makes the birds tweet.
The way I lick you'll be weak.
Oh! The taste is like a rocket up in space
It makes me feel like I'm in a great place.

Morgan Finlay (9)
St Ninian's RC Primary School, Livingston

Happiness

Happiness is the flowers in the back garden
So many lovely flowers, so many lovely colours.
Happiness is the smell of fresh air.
Happiness is the taste of fresh fruit.
Happiness is the moving water in the ocean.
Happiness is the sound of the animals.

Chantelle MacLean (8)
St Ninian's RC Primary School, Livingston

The Touch Poem

I like the touch of a lazy cat when it is lying down.
I like the touch of a cute puppy dog barking.
I like the touch of golden sand sliding through my hand.
I like the touch of soft fabric like clothes which I wear.
I like the touch of a big warm cuddle from my mummy.
I like the touch of fluffy wool when I am knitting.
I like the touch of slippery soap slipping in my hand.
I like the touch of soft flower petals swaying in the wind.

Becky Findlay (8)
St Ninian's RC Primary School, Livingston

Monkey

M onkeys are funny animals
O h-ooh ahh-ahh the monkeys sing
N o monkey hates bananas
K icking and swinging monkeys go
E very day's fun for them
Y elling at the top of their voices.

Keanu Sneddon (8)
St Ninian's RC Primary School, Livingston

What Is Green?

Green is the smell of newly fresh grass in spring.
Green is the sight of green glass beer bottles.
Green is the taste of green watery apples.
Green is the touch of a slithery snake.
Green is the sound of a frog croaking in the breeze.
Green is the touch of holly leaves rubbing against your face.

Alicia Turner (8)
St Ninian's RC Primary School, Livingston

Snow

Snow is white water
No one denies that soft snow is wonderful
Snow is soft, silver and cool
Water is frozen while snow is silver
Christmas cakes are tasty
Ripe robbers will never rob banks
Unless the bank is frozen like frozen foods
And finally the soft snow is gone.

Jordan More (12)
St Ninian's RC Primary School, Livingston

Friendship

Friendship is a balloon going over the moon,
I hope I hear from you soon,
Friendship is a rose just been watered.
Friendship is a bunny munching on a big orange carrot.
Friendship is a cute small puppy getting out for a walk.
Friendship is the best part of a milkshake.

Ariana Hardie (8)
St Ninian's RC Primary School, Livingston

What Is Blue?

Blue is the colour of the sea swirling on the beach.
Blue is as cold as an icicle on a winter's day.
Blue is the colour of a beautiful dolphin swimming in the sea.
Blue is the colour of a stream whizzing down the field.
Blue is the colour of the sky on a hot summer's day.

Sophie Wells (8)
St Ninian's RC Primary School, Livingston

Homework

My homework is always hard,
because my dog buried it in the backyard.

My pages are always crumbled,
my writing is always jumbled.

My jotters are all a mess
and my grades are always less.

Even when I'm in detention,
I always have to pay attention.

When I'm in the gym,
I always seem to tear a limb.

People feel a bit sorry for me,
because I have to watch educational TV.

At playtime I never have fun at all,
because I have to sweep the lunch hall.

I never have fun on Monday,
I wish it was Sunday

And to make matters worse,
some people say I have a curse.

So now do you see,
If you do your homework bad you could end up like me.

Lewis Mulholland (9)
St Ninian's RC Primary School, Livingston

Roman

R oman soldiers cross the land.
O n top of Celts.
M any armies were aggressive.
A ll that face the Romans shall
N ever face anyone again!

Cameron Russell (9)
St Ninian's RC Primary School, Livingston

Rainbows

Rainbows are all different colours
Like red, blue and green
Like yellow pink and purple
Nicest colours ever seen.

Rainbows are like cars
All different colours
Zooming down the road
Better than the others.

Rainbows are like pretty flowers
Like daisies and roses
They make lovely posies.

Rainbows are like butterflies
Colourful and bright
They even shine at night.

Keri Gibson (8)
St Ninian's RC Primary School, Livingston

Scotland

S cotland is a sunny place.
C astles are on volcanoes.
O ceans are cold, stormy and enormous.
T raditional food is haggis.
L andscapes are green.
A ll day will be great.
N ever leave Livingston
D ecember is cold and snowy.

Ciaran McWalter (8)
St Ninian's RC Primary School, Livingston

A Day In The Life Of An Eye

Woke up to see the beautiful glow of Earth's dawn,
I glanced outside at the blinding sun,
I could see blossoms falling off the tree.

Mum stood in the doorway but I couldn't understand what she said,
Mum making breakfast, I wish I could've smelt it but sadly, no.
Dad said something, tried to speak but no sound came out
                                    of my mouth.

Seeing people, places and things,
Nothing else,
Looking up, seeing the world,
But nothing else.

Saw home near,
Mum waiting at the door,
Looking at her, Dad there,
Tears filling my eyes,
They turned into a blue then disappeared,
A day in the life of an eye . . .

Geena Reilly
St Ninian's RC Primary School, Livingston

My Four Legged Friend

You wish you could, you may, you might meet my four legged friend.
He likes a tickle, a pat, a rub on the tummy, on the head, on the back
Most of all he likes to run, to hide, or jump and pick up sticks
He likes to chase a ball or the birds like he can fly . . .
He plays with me at hide and seek or jumps in my bed when it's still
                                    warm in the mornings.
But most of all he is my four legged friend
Who you would, you could meet and play with my four-legged friend.

Rhys Nixon (8)
St Ninian's RC Primary School, Livingston

Craziness

Craziness is hard to explain,
A bit like running about in an aeroplane.
Craziness is like crashing,
You will hear a lot of bashing.
Craziness is like a machine that never stops mashing,
You may be rushing . . . *to save the world,*
(Unlike my uncle Earl).
In the car park your car might be crushing.
Craziness is like running a mile,
Then jumping a stile.

Hugh Hardie (9)
St Ninian's RC Primary School, Livingston

What Is Purple?

Purple is a beautiful butterfly flapping in the wind.
Purple is a colour of oil with a blue and green tinge.
Purple is the colour I most admire.
Purple is a flower growing even higher.
Purple is a colour that is more beautiful than all the others.
Purple is a sunset painting the night sky.

Lauren Gilhooley (8)
St Ninian's RC Primary School, Livingston

Blue

Blue is a wave far out at sea which struggles to get to its tea
Blue is the colour of the sky
When blue is angry the waves start to swish
Blue is the ice on the pond which I would not go on
Blue is the colour of some lovely violets.

Aidan Craig (8)
St Ninian's RC Primary School, Livingston

A Raindrop

A raindrop is watery
It falls from the sky
It trickles down your face
And goes in your eyes
It's transparent and shiny
It changes colour.
Oh raindrop
Oh raindrop
You keep us alive.

Eilidh Clark (8)
St Ninian's RC Primary School, Livingston

Winter

In the green grass
There is silver sweet dew
All the gorgeous girls
And all the big boys
All play together
As friends.

Ciaran McNeil (10)
St Ninian's RC Primary School, Livingston

Love

It smells like a big cake,
It tastes like hot pies,
It sounds like a cat playing in the sun,
It feels like goodnight hugs,
It lives beside me.

Natasha Imrie (9)
St Ninian's RC Primary School, Livingston

Happiness

Happiness is blue like a shimmering swimming pool
It sounds like a person happily whistling to himself
Happiness tastes like a Galaxy bar
It smells like a white cube of chlorine floating in a swimming pool
Happiness feels like fluffy snow
It looks like a happy surfboarder riding on waves
Happiness reminds me of my little brother smiling up at me for
the first time.

Frank Declan McAlister (10)
St Ninian's RC Primary School, Livingston

Love Is . . .

Love is pink like a rose budding in the summer sun.
It sounds like a baby gurgling in its cot.
Love tastes like caramel, smooth and soft.
It smells like cherry blossoms falling off the trees.
Love looks like the stars twinkling in the midnight sky.
It feels like a bowl filled with feathers.
Love is . . .

Sheonaid Carlin (11)
St Ninian's RC Primary School, Livingston

Winter Fun

I love winter yes I do.
The cows in the snowy field go moo.
Silvery icicles hang from my nose.
I have been out so long my toes are numb.

Lee Francis McIlhone (10)
St Ninian's RC Primary School, Livingston

Love

It smells like the first day of summer,
It tastes like the wedding cake,
It sounds like church bells ringing,
It feels like love when they do the first dance,
It is happiness for me and you,
It is a playful day on summer bay,
It is true love for him and her,
It is love
And there is a tear in my eye,
My mum and dad,
It was on Monday because it was summer.

Natasha Reid (9)
St Ninian's RC Primary School, Livingston

Happiness

Happiness is as blue as crystal.
Happiness sounds like children playing.
Happiness tastes as sweet as strawberries.
Happiness smells like sweet flowers.
Happiness looks as wonderful as the midnight sky.
Happiness feels as special as a long holiday.
Happiness reminds me of my baby cousin.

James Alexander Bethell (11)
St Ninian's RC Primary School, Livingston

Love

Love is white as a lovely angel.
Love looks like beautiful flowers, yellow, orange and red.
Love sounds like the choir in the church singing songs.
Love tastes like the ice cream that you get in Paris.
Love smells like the wild berries.
Love reminds me of my wee cousin, Calum.

Robert McDonald (11)
St Ninian's RC Primary School, Livingston

Happiness

Happiness is sweet and smells like apples,
Happiness is nice and bright,
Happiness is magic on top of you,
Happiness is sweet with love,
Happiness is like a rainbow,
Happiness is the time to have love together,
Happiness is the time of your life to celebrate,
Happiness is a dog in love,
Happiness is a table with love.

Courtney Cook (10)
St Ninian's RC Primary School, Livingston

Happiness

Happiness is yellow like a smiley sun
Happiness tastes like strawberries, sweet as sugar
It sounds like baby bluebirds singing beautifully
It smells like a posy of pretty tulips pink, blue, yellow and red
Happiness looks like a choir of angels smiling down happily
It feels as soft as silk
Happiness reminds me of love
And everyone who loves me.

Annabelle Urquhart (10)
St Ninian's RC Primary School, Livingston

Joy

Joy is like a toy, joy can be a boy,
Joy is sad, joy is happy,
It tastes like chocolate,
It smells like happiness,
Joy is my favourite feeling,
It sounds like paper ripping,
It looks like a shiny piece of gold
And it can't let me stop speaking.

Ciaran Kelly (9)
St Ninian's RC Primary School, Livingston

Happiness

Happiness is cheerful, kindness spreads around,
Everybody's funny, sharing jokes,
Happiness is in the air, bugs happy,
The baker's smells of bread,
The sweetie shop smells like apple bonbons
And all I see is happy people, cheery pets, dogs and cats,
One house is very, very happy,
Four kids, one dog, one dad, one mum, two grans and grandas.

Joe Helanor (10)
St Ninian's RC Primary School, Livingston

Sadness

Sadness is baby blue, like tears trickling down red cheeks.
It feels like a broken heart travelling up your body.
Sadness tastes like fat at the very end of your steak.
It sounds like rain falling miserably onto the ground on
                                        a summer's day.
It smells like burnt chocolate on Valentine's Day.
Sadness reminds me of saying my last goodbyes to my cousin!

Lisa Harkins (11)
St Ninian's RC Primary School, Livingston

Happiness

Happiness is yellow like the burning bright sun.
It feels like dry sand, running through my hands.
Happiness looks like a golden piece of wheat.
It tastes like a mint ice cream on a hot day.
Happiness sounds like the fans at a football game.
It smells like Christmas turkey.
Happiness reminds me of the summer holidays.

Paul Ewins (11)
St Ninian's RC Primary School, Livingston

Happiness

Happiness feels like magic.
Happiness is very sweet.
Happiness tastes like lovely chocolate.
Happiness sounds nice and kind and makes me feel happy,
Happiness is a time when everyone has a lovely smile on their face.
Happiness is when everyone is talking to each other.
Happiness is sweet and juicy.
Happiness is playing together.

Martin Hughes (9)
St Ninian's RC Primary School, Livingston

Craziness!

Craziness is weird and wonderful,
It smells like perfume just from the tin,
It tastes like chocolate all melted and creamy,
It sounds like sweet music from the recorder,
It feels like a sponge cake all soft and delicate,
It lives underneath you so watch out!

Jane Ewins (9)
St Ninian's RC Primary School, Livingston

If I Were

If I were a bird I would fly high over the mountain like a jet,
If I were a mouse I would creep about the house,
If I were a cat I would never take my eye off that rat
And if I were a rabbit I would hop around the wood like a spring.

Daniel Rolfe (9)
St Ninian's RC Primary School, Livingston

Happiness

The sky is blue, the sun is bright,
I am smiling,
I am funny,
I am sad,
I am lonely, that's why I didn't want to stay.
There is the moon coming out to play,
I can hear the foxes howling,
It is dark, I am sad,
I am still happy today.

Rhiannon Cairns (9)
St Ninian's RC Primary School, Livingston

Guss

My name is Guss,
The chimneysweep,
I'm as sharp as a thistle,
As small as a tistle,
So put a scarf around my neck
And . . . go on then, give me a little peck,
Don't let the dust go in my eye,
Because I'm not in the sky,
Now I just need to say goodbye.

Liam Mackay (9)
St Ninian's RC Primary School, Livingston

Courage

Courage is bravery
It smells like the Second World War,
It tastes like the death on the battlefield,
It sounds like the shouts of victory,
It feels like the armour they wore,
It lives through the wind where death had struck,
For soldiers whose lives had run out of luck.

Anna Whyte (9)
St Ninian's RC Primary School, Livingston

Happiness

Happiness is sweet and kind,
Happiness tastes like a juice from the cup,
Happiness is nice and loving,
Happiness is going places together,
Happiness is playing together with my gran's dog,
Happiness is going for a walk with my best friend,
Happiness is fun and a good day,
Happiness feels like magic.

Louise Ann McDonald (9)
St Ninian's RC Primary School, Livingston

Snowdrops

Snowdrops are falling so slow
Like the winter glow.
Snowdrops look so nice
Like little white mice.
Snowdrops are like new flowers
And have millions of powers.
Snowdrops are white
And it is a beautiful sight.

Kayleigh Murray (9)
St Ninian's RC Primary School, Livingston

Happiness

Happiness is pink,
It smells like beautiful flowers,
It tastes like a big chocolate ice cream,
It sounds like cute birds singing,
It feels like my two puppies,
They live at my nana's.

Ronnie Anne Jarvie (9)
St Ninian's RC Primary School, Livingston

A Girl's Summer

Flips flops, belly tops,
Lemonade in the shade,
Blue skies, hot guys,
Late nights, water fights,
Ice cream, sweet dreams,
Party time, lookin' fine,
Sleepin' in, sneakin' out,
That's what girls are all about!

Ayeisha Mohammed (9)
St Ninian's RC Primary School, Livingston

Love

Everyone knows the nice side of love,
Now for the *bad*.
It will rip your heart to shreds.
Love is so evil,
It will take your heart and life.
Any person could mistake love,
Just like . . . you!

Victoria Price (9)
St Ninian's RC Primary School, Livingston

Caring

C are for the poor
A nd don't let them die
R unning away and not helping is really hurtful
I 'd give them money to help them
N ever leave a lonely child by itself
G ather toys for the poor.

Kirsty Lamb (8)
St Ninian's RC Primary School, Livingston

Winter Poem

W inter is a nice snowing season
I t is good fun to play in the snowy place.
N ever wake up on Christmas Eve because Santa comes
on Christmas Eve.
T ime to go and play in the snow.
E verything is covered in ice.
'R est,' said the snowman as he fell.

Michael Ian Caskie (8)
St Ninian's RC Primary School, Livingston

My Acrostic Poem Of Caring

C aring is a really good thing
A nd it helps people
R emember to be nice to everyone
I n poor countries and give money
N ever ignore sick, poor and old people
G ive money, games and toys to poor children.

Lauren Gausden (9)
St Ninian's RC Primary School, Livingston

The Roman Poem

R omans ruled Britain
O ver hills and seas
M any Romans hated Scotland
A nd then they decided to make a wall
N ever break the wall.

Ahsaan Razaq (8)
St Ninian's RC Primary School, Livingston

Untitled

When the hot sun shines
Children are at play
Making sandcastles
Doing it their own way

Sun is blazing in the sky
Children swim in the pool
Doing backstroke
Acting like they are so cool

I go to the beach
Get an ice cream
Play in the sea
I see the sun beam

Time to go home
The sun has gone down
We all feel tired
Tourists are all over town.

Luke Borthwick (8)
St Ninian's RC Primary School, Livingston

Roman

R omans have a lot of money.
O nly lady Romans don't go to war.
M any of the Romans died in a war.
A ll of the Romans took over Britain.
N ever fight with a Roman.

Tara Mahmood (9)
St Ninian's RC Primary School, Livingston

When The Sun Shines

When the sun shines
People come out
Winter is over
Without a doubt

The sun is hot
Your ice cream melts
Get hit by a beach ball
Look what's on the barbecue belts
Pick up a shell
Play on the beach
Running a marathon
Drink water with a peach
Have an éclair
Animals come out of hibernation
So you can stroke a mare

Sun is setting
Very quick
It's turning to night
In a flick.

Matt Stephenson (9)
St Ninian's RC Primary School, Livingston

Romans

R uthless Romans
O nly some survived
M any Romans were killed
A ggressive Romans were good fighters
N ever argue with Romans.

Zainab Rehman (8)
St Ninian's RC Primary School, Livingston

Winter Acrostic Poem

W hite snow covers the Earth and
I ce covers the pond
N ew snowmen are built
T hunder strikes against the houses
E vacuating animals go to hibernate
R ustling trees have lost their leaves.

Christopher Neilson (9)
St Ninian's RC Primary School, Livingston

Caring

C an you help
A child who is
R ummaging for food
I nside the bins
N ot successfully
G ood and happy things can happen if you help them.

James Dawson (9)
St Ninian's RC Primary School, Livingston

The Romans

R omans conquered
O ver Britain
M any Celts fought Romans
A nd
N ow are dead.

Romaan Babar (9)
St Ninian's RC Primary School, Livingston

My Winter Poem

W inter wonderland is here.
 I nsane snow begins.
N ever stopping again.
T errible blizzards come from the sky.
E verlasting ice outside.
R isky frost on the road.

Aneesa Dastgir (9)
St Ninian's RC Primary School, Livingston

Caring

C aring for the poor
A nd being helpful to the old people
R emember to help the disabled
 I f you see someone who is hurt, help them
N ot making fun of them
G ive money to the poor.

Storm Imrie (9)
St Ninian's RC Primary School, Livingston

Windy

W ind is fun outside
 I fly my kite today.
N ow it's even windier.
D own fall the yellow tears.
Y ears pass and the wind is still there.

Iona-Marie Callaghan (7)
St Ninian's RC Primary School, Livingston

Windy

W ind make me fly
 I fly my kite
N ow we can play in the wind
D ay two all my friends are inside
Y ears pass, it is still windy.

Rose Ewins (7)
St Ninian's RC Primary School, Livingston

Windy

W ind is cold let's get dizzy now.
 I nside you can hear the wind blow.
N ow we can play in the wind.
D ad gets ready now.
Y ey, let's play in the wind.

Stephanie Nixon (7)
St Ninian's RC Primary School, Livingston

Windy

W indy days are cold
 I want to play outside
N early time to go home
D own fall the leaves
Y ellow leaves.

Sean Imrie (8)
St Ninian's RC Primary School, Livingston

Windy

W hen it is windy
  I fly my kite.
N ext, let's jump in the
D eep leaves, one, two, three
Y ippee, it is fun playing in the wind.

Taylor Hogg (7)
St Ninian's RC Primary School, Livingston

Welcome Acrostic

W elcome to Scotland.
E veryone is kind and loving here.
L iving here is so much fun.
C ome and live here with us.
O pening doors to you is great.
M any people who come never want to go back.
E ach of you special people will realise that we are special too.

Anya Vitaliev (8)
St Peter's Primary School, Edinburgh

Welcome Acrostic

W elcome to Scotland, see the waves welcome.
E ach person is a Scot.
L augh out loud, have some fun.
C ome to Scotland, be my friend.
O pen your eyes, look up.
M y friends are all around you
E very day people are arriving.

Mhairi-Claire McGowan (8)
St Peter's Primary School, Edinburgh

Welcome Acrostic

W elcome to Scotland
E verybody can be friends with each other
L iving together as neighbours
C ome to Scotland, see Loch Ness
O ld days are past, so we can start afresh
M y friend is from Sri Lanka and I am trying to welcome her
E very day people should treat people the same way as they
treat others.

Molly Keenan (8)
St Peter's Primary School, Edinburgh

Welcome Acrostic

W elcome to a great place, Scotland
E veryone is friendly here
L oving is Scotland's favourite word
C ome and have fun
O ther people will learn quickly here
M ore fun to do here
E verything is gorgeous here.

Neave Keenan (8)
St Peter's Primary School, Edinburgh

Welcome Acrostic

W e would like to welcome new Scots
E ven if they are different races
L ots of Scots have come from different countries
C ome to Scotland, we always have room for you
O ld times a past gone so let's start afresh
M ore people, more fun
E veryone can become a Scot.

Alessia Pasquariello (8)
St Peter's Primary School, Edinburgh

Welcome Acrostic

W elcome to fabulous Scotland
E veryone is welcome here
L oving is nice
C aring for people is a way of welcoming them
O ther people from other countries should not be treated badly
M ay people care and love and help other people who are new
E veryone should have a very good life.

Elissa Hasson (8)
St Peter's Primary School, Edinburgh

Welcome Acrostic

W elcome to Scotland
E very day we play together
L oving each other and caring
C ome and stay for a day
O pen your eyes and see
M arvellous things happen here
E very day we're welcoming.

Sinéad Millar (8)
St Peter's Primary School, Edinburgh

Welcome Acrostic

W elcome to Edinburgh and Scotland.
E veryone welcomes you.
L iving in Edinburgh is great!
C ome to Scotland or Edinburgh.
O nly it is really hygienic and Eco friendly.
M any people in Scotland and Edinburgh
E ach one of us is special.
    Everyone is welcome.

Marcus Corrigan (8)
St Peter's Primary School, Edinburgh

Welcome Acrostic

W elcome to Scotland, we are enjoying it.
E veryone can come to this wonderful place.
L iving in Scotland is very nice.
C ome and have lots of fun.
O nly Scotland is a very cold place.
M any people like Scotland.
E very person comes to Scotland and has lots of fun

Matthew Laurie (8)
St Peter's Primary School, Edinburgh

Welcome Acrostic

W elcome to Scotland
E veryone in Scotland is really nice
L iving in Scotland is great
C ome to live in Scotland, it's great
O nly people with smiles are allowed
M any people are kind
E ach person will be welcomed.

Mairi Mulvanny (8)
St Peter's Primary School, Edinburgh

Welcome Acrostic

W elcome to Scotland
E verything is great
L oving people all around you
C ome and join in all the fun
O ther people come and settle
M any come from all around
E very one of us welcome.

Eilidh Buchan (8)
St Peter's Primary School, Edinburgh

Bullying Poem

When will they get me?
They find me everywhere I go.
Where are they?
They are always hiding.

Why do they wait for me?
- To get me
I want to say stop
But I am too scared.

How do they do it?
By intimidating me
Why do they do it?
Because they are bullies.

Peter Blair (11)
St Peter's Primary School, Edinburgh

Spring

Spring is when the shoots burst up
And the flowers begin to bloom,
The trees go pink with the blossom,
Saying that summer will be here soon!

The days get longer and warmer,
The grass grows long and green,
The place is so crowded with flowers,
Sometimes you cannot be seen!

Niamh Jarvis (9)
St Peter's Primary School, Edinburgh

My Own Special Skin

My dad is black,
My mum is white
And that is why I have my own special skin.

I've always known I was different,
I've always felt I was special,
Although, to my displeasure
I was treated as though I wasn't
At school . . .

It all started when
The new girl came,
She was big and blonde
With beautiful blue eyes.
She was pretty
And quickly became popular,
That's when I lost my friends who have black skin.

I smiled
And said hi to her.
She laughed and looked,
With pity.

The next day she came up to me
And she said hi to me,
Using the accent I use.
I nervously bit my fingernail
And wondered.

Later that day, she skipped in front of me,
In the lunch queue.
I looked at her,
She said, 'Is something wrong?'
I didn't understand,
Though I knew something
Wasn't right.

At the end of school,
I rushed quickly home,
I wanted to see my dad.
She followed me . . .
And tried to grab my bus fare.
At this moment she was alone,
It was the best time to sort it out,
And we did, we are friends now and I am proud,
Of my own special skin.

Charlotte McGowan (11)
St Peter's Primary School, Edinburgh

The Big Bad Dream

A crash of thunder
A scream of pain
As a sword is driven
Through the roof of your mouth.
A flash of light
As you are ripped apart
Limb by limb.
A gasp and blackness
Crushing in all around you.
A madman, a knife in his hand.
He throws it!
You wake up drenched in sweat
Afraid to fall into
The big, bad dream.

Patrick Mulvanny (10)
St Peter's Primary School, Edinburgh

That Day

It was two months ago,
That day,
But it seems just like yesterday,
The day the bullies came for me.
The day I was beaten to their hearts' content.

At first I thought it was just an intimidating glare,
Until his gang teased me about my skin,
I tried to shout back,
'How would you like it if I teased you about your skin?'
But that just made them angrier with me.

I tried to tell a teacher,
But they said, 'You dare,'
And I just ran away.

But they didn't give up.
They came for me
And trapped me in a corner.
This is it, I thought to myself.
As the leader rolled up his sleeves,
He had a gruesome look on his face.

I saw a fist smashing towards my face,
Before everything went completely blank.

Later I found myself lying on the path,
I had a horrible taste of blood in my mouth
And I was aching in agonising pain.

With very great care,
I picked myself up from the ground
And limped my way home,
Where in my bedroom I wept myself to sleep.

When I woke up that morning
And went for a shower,
I found myself covered in bruises
And I found a strong urge inside me,
I knew what to do.

I went to school the next day,
Still in real pain,
I went up to the teacher
And I gulped.

I told her about the bullies
And everything was,
Great!

Rian McDermott (11)
St Peter's Primary School, Edinburgh

Victim Of The City

I am a United supporter,
Everyone else likes City,
But I don't care,
I don't like their fans.

When I go to a match,
I hate the songs they sing.
The way they look at me,
I don't like their fans.

Maybe they have fun,
Taunting and teasing me.
I wish I were someone else,
I don't like their fans.

I feel all alone,
In the big world.
I go to no more matches,
I just don't like their fans.

That's just me.
Victim of the City.

Kieran FitzGerald (11)
St Peter's Primary School, Edinburgh

Little Claire

I used to be a bully
A mean and selfish girl
Who never understood the yelling
And tears of children
Just like me . . .

That was before
Before I met little Claire.

I thought she was helpless
Sad with no friends
She was small with blonde curly hair
And blue eyes.

I gazed down at her
I saw fear in her eyes
I didn't care.
'Give me your lunch money!'
I said putting my tough voice on.

As she reached into her bag
I saw her hand stop
Suddenly her voice said
'No!'
'Give me your lunch money or I'll -'
She interrupted me with a stern voice
'Get your own lunch money.'

Those five little words changed me for life.
I never bullied again, not after little Claire
And suddenly I was the only one who was left out
And not allowed to play.

I never forgot little Claire,
She was the only one who told me
To stop!

Sally Cairns (11)
St Peter's Primary School, Edinburgh

Running

A small dark-skinned girl,
Running with her friends.
Wait . . .
Running away from them.

Five mean, angry boys,
Chasing a little girl.
Running like a gale,
Gaining fast on her.

The small dark-skinned girl,
Comes to a dead end.
Fear like a dark hole closing up,
The girl starts to tremble and cry.

Those heartless bullies,
Attacking the girl.
Pain like being pierced with long, sharp swords,
Agony, sadness.

Little girl feeling small,
Hiding from those intimidating boys.
Anger like an active volcano,
It is just dark skin.

Those mean, aggressive boys again,
Annoying the girl.
Think,
Now can I help her?

The poor little girl,
Being teased so cruelly.
Stop!
Leave her alone now.

Running,
The *boys* are running away now.
A small dark-skinned girl,
Experiences happiness.

Tom Jarvis (11)
St Peter's Primary School, Edinburgh

Another Day

It is the end of
Another day
Name-calling
Punching
Being laughed at.

I am lying
On the floor
Blood
Dripping from my nose.
The blood is salty
It tastes horrible.

Why me?
I don't understand
It's not my fault
I'm black, an Ethiopian.

I am on my way
Home
At my front door
I am scared
What will my mother say?
She might tell the teacher
Then what?
Then the teacher will
Give Mary a row
A telling off
Then what will she do to
Me?

I walk in
My mother makes a fuss
I say I don't want to talk about it
The truth is I do
But I fear
It will get me in more trouble.

I go to my room
I cry my eyes out
I am so sad
What am I to do?
I fall asleep
Wondering and wondering
What am I to do?

It is a new day
I am slowly getting ready
For school
Dreading going into school . . .

Mary's there waiting for me
I am shaking
My knees knocking against each other.

All of a sudden
I shout, 'Leave me alone!'
She looks scared herself
She walks away.

I feel great
I am walking home from school
With no blood or fear for
The next day
I've got an amazing
Burst of excitement inside of me.

Tomorrow is going to be
A new day.

Anna Service (11)
St Peter's Primary School, Edinburgh

The Fact Remains . . .

Inside my eyes,
The awful din,
Torments my mind,
From scalp to chin.
Is this my doing?
Is this my fault?
Have my actions provoked these taunts?

Beneath my crown of curly hair,
I question their motives,
This isn't fair!
They judge me by my race, my skin,
Regardless of the heart within.
I've grown immune to constant threats.
My parents' response - Mum worries, Dad frets.

The bullies are fierce, mean, deluded,
Who now attempt to fix their wrongs,
Undo the aggression they once exuded.
But nothing now to ease the pain,
The memories of their gruesome game,
Though sadly still, the fact remains,
You can't undo the laws of fate.
I'll never return to my former state.

Francis Kerrigan (11)
St Peter's Primary School, Edinburgh

The Day The Tables Turned

I hear them coming,
I turn . . .
To check,
It is them,
I turn back and run,
I carry on running,
Until I can't hear them,
I turn . . .
There they are again,
I dash like a cheetah, to get away,
I go round a corner and lean against the wall,
I take a deep breath
And peek timidly round the corner,
There they are . . .
In a circle,
They were after someone else,
I have to stop them,
I march towards the circle
And lead the person out,
The gang stare in amazement and run off,
They never bother me again.
Ever!

Tom Linklater (11)
St Peter's Primary School, Edinburgh

Our Hearts Beat Together

Inside my head I am full of terrifying thoughts,
Behind my eyes I am filled with fright and shock.

We are one, our hearts beat together.

Beneath my skin I feel hatred and dislike,
Behind my ears, it's sore when they bite.

We are one, our hearts beat together.

My tears fill up my eyes, I feel so scared.
They can strike anywhere, I am so unprepared.

We are one, our hearts beat together.

Finally you've stopped, you've realised what you've done.

Our hearts are happy, they beat together as one.

Melissa Lugton Laurie (11)
St Peter's Primary School, Edinburgh

Why?

Why does she pick on me? I've done nothing wrong
It gives her some power if I don't belong.

Why does she laugh when my eyes fill with tears?
Because bullies like her thrive on worry and fear.

Why do her words hurt me so bad?
Her words eat my heart and that makes her glad.

Why does she pounce on a deserted street?
Because then no one hears my struggling feet.

Why doesn't she say sorry for ruining my life?
Because to her that would be admitting she's a coward inside.

Chloe Bruce-Gardyne (11)
St Peter's Primary School, Edinburgh

Fear

Inside my head,
I'm filled with fear,
Thoughts in my head,
Burst into bubbles,
Everyone has its nasty name,
All day long playing their chilling game.

Beneath my ribs,
My heart pounds,
Like a *tick, tick, ticking* of the clock,
Then it gets faster,
As the clock strikes another chapter.

Under my skin,
I feel punches,
It makes me feel like a rock,
Constantly being cursed by rapid waves.

The smell of fear all around,
I dread the corners of the playground.

Kathleen O'Dwyer (12)
St Peter's Primary School, Edinburgh

I'm Not Afraid

Ever since primary 1
I have been bullied.
As the years went on
The bullies never changed.
They steal my lunch money
And I get in trouble.
They hide my gym bag
And I don't get to do PE.
Then I realised this would never end,
So I shouted at the bullies and said,
'I'm not afraid of you!'
And the bullies never bullied me again.

Ryan Lannie (11)
St Peter's Primary School, Edinburgh

The Bullies Are Back

Last term I met the bullies,
They took my coat and shoes,
Pulling my red hair is their favourite,
I used to love my hair, but that all changed,
My mum really likes it.
Oh why can't I change my hair?

This term I met them again,
I hid in the toilets in my new shoes,
I told Mum not to buy them,
The bell rang.
I ran to the classroom and there they were,
They looked so big and frightening.

I felt sore kicks under the table,
The bell for break rang,
My heart started to race,
The tallest, Rachel came nearer,
She took me into a corner,
My heart nearly broke with fear.

She didn't get a chance to do anything,
We all went back to the classroom,
I finally got the courage to tell,
I told on them!
The teacher could now deal with them,
I felt so good,
I now enjoy school.

Gillian Reid (11)
St Peter's Primary School, Edinburgh

The Gang

Here they come!
The gang of bullies
I was scared of them
Everybody was, no one liked them
Even their parents and teachers didn't like them

Everyone was always well away from them
Their leader, Bob
Trampled forward
Whose fault was it
That I was Pakistani?
Just because I am a different colour of skin
Doesn't mean I am not as good

If I were white would that mean
I'd get treated differently?
But then I decided to stand up to them
One of the funniest things I have ever seen
Was Bob's face
He was absolutely shocked
That somebody stood up to him
I walked home with my head held high
I was delighted.

Michael Monan (11)
St Peter's Primary School, Edinburgh

Under Our Bones

Inside my head
My thoughts are swimming
They are trapped in a bottle
But the cork won't come out.

Beneath my ears
The drums are beating
As I struggle to stamp out all the ugly remarks
That have flooded my confidence.

I don't understand
For we are the same
Under our bones.

Behind my eyes
I sting with fear
The picture is a blur
With all the tears . . .
I don't want to look back.

I don't understand
For we are the same
Under our bones.

Inside my head
My mind is debating
Should I tell, no
If I were to tell
I would feel the weight
Of threat looming by my side,
Or would I?
They may stop
And then I would feel
The threat of fear disintegrating
Into the depths of Hell.

I don't understand
Why do I feel like this?
I shouldn't.
After all, we are the same
Under our bones.

Lisa Wilson (11)
St Peter's Primary School, Edinburgh

Bullies Don't Care

Her hard, pink fist
Beats against my soft, black cheek
It hurts, like an animal eating me alive
But she doesn't care

I have no friends to help me
She has a gang
They're terrifying and aggressive
But they don't care

I try getting up
She only beats me down again
I want to go home
But nobody cares

My heart beats inside my chest
Her elbows beat against my chest
I'm crying
But I don't care

As I try once more to get up
She walks away
I shout at her
Now she cares

I am back on my feet
One of her gang swings a punch
I block it with my arm
Now they care

Everyone wonders how I did it
Beat the bullies
I stood up for myself
Now everybody cares

There's no more bullies
No more fighting
I'm happy
Now I care.

Anya MacSorley-Pringle (11)
St Peter's Primary School, Edinburgh

Looking Through Their Eyes

I try to penetrate those cold fierce eyes that penetrate mine
so strongly.
I try to find a route into that well protected fortress.
But then I find my only way is by looking through their eyes.

Through my nerves the pain is etched, it never really leaves me.
Every morning I wake up sore and know to expect tenfold at noon,
I try to gain access to those rough walls that are home to my pain,
But I realise the only way in, is by looking though their eyes.

Under me is the unthinkable, a network of pain that cannot
be described.
In me is an empty castle, it stays standing for so long.
I look for a weak spot in my enemy and then I realise the only way
in is through looking through their eyes.

Everything is crashing down all around me. My one defence is gone,
I wait for the inevitable crushing of my soul and the everlasting pain.
But wait, I look into those eyes and then I see it.

Pain beyond mine . . .

Sean Frost (11)
St Peter's Primary School, Edinburgh

Behind My Brain

Behind my brain my thoughts feel the sorrowful grip of memories
Behind my brain the livid words fill my tormented head.

Behind my brain my heart is torn to a million shreds
Behind my brain my eyes are blinded by the spit of horror.

Behind my brain my head tries to forget my misery
Behind my brain is a house of questions.

Stephen Dolan (11)
St Peter's Primary School, Edinburgh

The Person You Can't See

Inside my head all hope deteriorates
Of me ever escaping their evil grasps, oh so cunning,
Around me the nasty comments swirl (around me)
Yet I desperately try to block them out.
My muscles are screaming, tired from running
But I can't stop now they're still about.

Inside my eyes, tears begin to dwell
Making my eyesight blurry
Beneath my head of hair lies a mind of dark, sad memories.
Dark. Dark. Dark.
Around me the night draws near. I have to hurry.
I wish I had a friend to play with, laugh with and have a lark.

Behind the dark eyes you think you know
The kids you pick on. Well hey, you're not so clever.
When the fear in me grows and grows
I just wish black and white would be happy together.

Anna McNairney (11)
St Peter's Primary School, Edinburgh

Under My Skin

Under my heart *beep! Beep! Beep!* Where are its pretty colours?
Pink and *red,* where's the loveliness, huh?

Under my head, in my brain, there are little balls fuzzing about in pain.
When will they stop?
Stop! Stop! Stop! I chorus in my head.

Under my wrists I feel like I am going to die.
The bullies pressed so, so hard my blood feels different from usual.

Under my stomach is pain.
From when they hung me upside down, I feel so dizzy
I know I am about to faint.

Under my thoughts is worry and me the poor, poor victim.

Sophie McKenzie (11)
St Peter's Primary School, Edinburgh

Feelings

My feelings are as dark and as cold as a cave in winter.
Thanks to him.
Behind my eyes the everlasting images have to be locked away
in a safe.

Thanks to him.

Shame and fear passes by me like a late train to Dunfermline.
Thanks to him.
Beneath my skin I can feel a cold hand crushing my soul.
Thanks to him.
This mocking it can't be doing me any good, the pain is killing
me inside.

Thanks to him.

Sophie Watson (11)
St Peter's Primary School, Edinburgh

To A Bully

Why do you hurt me in every single way?
Why do you hurt me every single day?

I don't like it; it's not fun,
You'll have no friends, so it is dumb.

I would stop if I were you,
I have friends; don't you want some too?

I am not scared of you,
I am not scared.
Hurting is not the way to go;
So change now!

Peter Rennie (11)
St Peter's Primary School, Edinburgh

Dogs

Dogs can be big or small,
Labradors, retrievers
And miniature schnauzers . . .
We love them all.
Terries have an awful bite,
Collies have a very good sight,
Dalmatian dogs are spotty
And toy poodles are naughty,
Some dogs bite, some dogs don't,
Don't be afraid of a man's best friend.

Paige Watson (11)
Stobhill Primary School

The Pigs, The Cat And The Mouse

Once upon a time
In a land called Dine
There lived a pig called Sam
But his big fear was to become sliced ham.

A fairy went to his house
Looking for the killer mouse
The mouse was killed
And Sam was thrilled.

Sam's pig brother Ben
Built himself a pen
But a wicked old cat
Made the pen all flat.

Rory Hardie (8)
The Mary Erskine & Stewart's Melville Junior School

The Clock Tower

Once upon a time
A clock tower chimed
Out popped four little snouts
The clock struck twelve
And four little elves
Ran out with twinkling bells.

Off to the shop
The little elves hopped
Looking to help the shoemaker
They hammered and sewed
Till the hot sun rose
Then rushed back to the clock tower safely.

The shoemaker was surprised
He shouted out and cried
So he put out some tea for his helpers
The elves returned dancing
Hammered and sewed, prancing
And everyone lived happily ever after.

Juliet Anderson (8)
The Mary Erskine & Stewart's Melville Junior School

The Viking Who Wanted To Grow

There once was a Viking from Oslo
Who really just wanted to fast grow,
So he sailed far away
In search of Special K,
But the only thing growing was his big toe.

Ben Voy (8)
The Mary Erskine & Stewart's Melville Junior School

Bert With His Shirt

There once was a Viking called Bert
He said, 'Oh, this armour does hurt
I can stand it no more
I'll nip down to the store
And I'll buy a soft, colourful shirt.'

He tried the shirt on
But the sleeves were too long
From his head to his toe
His tights did not show;
Bert had the sizing all wrong

And you know that men don't care
About the clothes that they wear
Be it armour or shirt
Whether clean or with dirt
But Bert does, because he's now bare!

Emma Yau (8)
The Mary Erskine & Stewart's Melville Junior School

The Viking's Dance

There was a young Viking from Oslo
Who liked to put on a pink bolero
He danced day and night
From dawn's first light
Then auditioned for a part as a solo.

Sophie Jenkins (8)
The Mary Erskine & Stewart's Melville Junior School

The Mighty Viking

There was a mighty Viking
Whose name was Mick of Might
He sailed the seas rough and smooth
In battle he would fight.

His sword was bright and strong
But his crew gave off a pong
They would not bath, day or night
So they always looked a fright.

As they were sailing back
They soon were under attack
They killed them all
And had a ball
But their boat began to crack.

The boat began to sink
The Vikings fell into the drink
There was blood and guts
And such a fuss
In the future they should stop and think.

Cameron Bowie (8)
The Mary Erskine & Stewart's Melville Junior School

The Viking From Oslo

There once was a Viking from Oslo
Who at a show sang a solo
He sailed far away
Because of dismay
At the show, he sang the song too slow.

Eilidh McGoldrick (8)
The Mary Erskine & Stewart's Melville Junior School

Mary The Pig Fairy

In the beautiful beautiful moonlight
The big clock struck midnight
And thousands of fairies were flying about
One was part pig and had a pig snout

Her name was Mary Flutterwings
She collected shells and other things
And she had had a curse put on
By a wicked witch, now gone

Only by the magic Fairy Queen
Could the curse be undone, if seen
So she flew to the palace far away
Hoping Queen could undo it in a day

The palace was sparkling and pink
And colours that you cannot think
The Queen waved her magical wand
And snout and tail soon were gone.

Rachel Lind (9)
The Mary Erskine & Stewart's Melville Junior School

Dolphins

There was a dolphin named Star,
Who liked to go to the bar,
He drank some gold beer
And gave a huge cheer,
Then said, 'Do you have a car?'

Zoë Adams (8)
The Mary Erskine & Stewart's Melville Junior School

In The Days Of The Vikings

In the days of nine hundred and fifty
The Vikings were very, very nifty
Their axes were sharp
But they all hated the harp
And their dancing was very shifty

They invented longboats
And stylish raiding coats
And helmets all shiny and strong
They were not tall or short
But when dancing they tended to snort

They loved to dance
To spin and prance
They were good at jazz and tap
And they did a really good rap
But they danced in vests and pants!

Now they are gone
But their legend lives on
Forever and a day
'Up hello Aa!' you hear them shout
And their dancing goes down a storm.

Michael Holmes (8)
The Mary Erskine & Stewart's Melville Junior School

The Viking Who Wanted To Go Hiking

There once was a thin and tall Viking
Who went to a mountain to go hiking
He sailed far away
And had a delay
So he ended up going motor biking.

Sophie Jane Lawrence (9)
The Mary Erskine & Stewart's Melville Junior School

Best Friends

B est friends never break up
E veryone should be friends
S haring sweets and toys
T elling each other secrets

F orever we play
R iding on roller coasters together
I n the hot sun
E veryone together
N o need to fall out
D efinitely friends
S miling all the time.

Amy Deas (10)
The Royal High Primary School

Harvest - Haikus

Harvest, harvest move
You need to get harvested
We have to move now

Harvest, harvest please
Time is not on our side
We need to hurry

Harvest, harvest rest
We have to rest for next year
Rest, rest harvest, rest.

Heather Notman (9)
The Royal High Primary School

Best Friends

B est friends forever
E verywhere we play
S leepovers all the time
T ill we get tired

F riends forever
R iding together
I n the sea
E verywhere we play
N o falling out
D oing fun things when the
S un follows us.

Megan Abigail Young (9)
The Royal High Primary School

Dancing

D ancing is my favourite thing
A nd so is skiing too
N ow dance, come on
C an you dance to the beat
I know I can
N ow dance, come on
G o go.

Mhari Campbell (9)
The Royal High Primary School

My Socks

My socks became famous on stage
Then one day they died of old age
When children heard they were sad
And some went totally mad
If only they hadn't died of old age.

Ross McKenzie (9)
The Royal High Primary School

Winter

I really hate the wind and rain,
It makes me sad, it's such a pain,
I much prefer the summer sun,
When I go out and play and have some fun.

In the spring the flowers are nice and bright,
The moon doesn't come out till later at night,
In autumn the leaves start falling down,
It's getting near winter, that makes me frown!

Chloe Taylor Campbell (9)
The Royal High Primary School

Chelsea

C arling Cup winners that's what we are
H eroes, the players from near and far
E very player always giving their best
L eague champions that's us beating the rest
S tamford Bridge is where we play
E ach fan makes their way
A vram Grant in the dugout on match day.

Curtis Laydon (9)
The Royal High Primary School

Young Writers Information

We hope you have enjoyed reading this book - and that you will continue to enjoy it in the coming years.

If you like reading and writing poetry drop us a line, or give us a call, and we'll send you a free information pack.

Alternatively if you would like to order further copies of this book or any of our other titles, then please give us a call or log onto our website at www.youngwriters.co.uk

Young Writers Information
Remus House
Coltsfoot Drive
Peterborough
PE2 9JX

(01733) 890066